WOMEN MADE NEW

Reflections on Adversity, Transformation, and Healing

Compiled by Crystalina Evert

EWTN Publishing, Inc.
Irondale, Alabama

EWTN Publishing, Inc.
5817 Old Leeds Road, Irondale, AL 35210

Distributed by Sophia Institute Press, Box 5284, Manchester, NH 03108.

hardcover ISBN 978-1-68278-289-7

ebook ISBN 978-1-68278-290-3

Library of Congress Control Number: 2022941610

First printing

Dedicated to Mother Angelica

Prayer

Lord Jesus, You know the pain we have when we're disappointed: disappointed in those we loved when we found they did not love us in return; disappointed in things and people and everything and everyone. We're disappointed sometimes in the world and those around us, disappointed in ourselves. We place all of the disappointments, Lord, in Your Sacred Heart and the Immaculate Heart of Mary. We place them as in a furnace of love that You possess. Sacred Heart of Jesus and Immaculate Heart of Mary, my sweet Mother, mend all who suffer disappointment and place them in Your Sacred Hearts; give them the courage to stand tall, to persevere, and to trust in Your wondrous providence—that providence that is always present, always there. Amen.

CONTENTS

Foreword by Rev. Louis M. Solcia ix

1. Unbroken by Crystalina Evert 2

2. Regret, Remorse, and Sorrow by Mother Angelica 12

3. "Surrender" Is Not a Four-Letter Word by Teresa Tomeo . . 26

4. Beauty by Fr. Joseph Mary Wolfe, MFVA 46

5. Whom Shall I Please? by Catherine Hadro 58

6. Living within the Fiats by Sr. Bethany Madonna, SV . . 70

7. Changes by Joy Pinto 86

8. Breaking Free by Crystalina Evert 96

9. Space for Grace by Dr. Kymberly Scipione 108

10. He's Lying to You by Cameron Fradd. 116

11. The Feminine Genius by Lisa Cotter 128

12. Divorce Hurts More Than Two by Leila Miller 140

13. We Are Women at the Well by Sarah Swafford 164

14. Who Are You? by Johnnette B. Williams 174

15. Be Aware of Your Battle by Crystalina Evert 190

16. People in Personal Prisons by Mother Angelica 200

Letter to Women by Crystalina Evert 215

Inspiration from Scripture 217

About the Author 222

About the Contributors 223

FOREWORD

I have known Crystalina for twenty years and have been her spiritual director. I married Jason and Crystalina, baptized their children, and watched them grow over the years.

I have seen the good times and bad times that all people experience in their lives. All too often, we want to give up when problems arise, but indeed, there are no problems—only solutions! It comes down to not giving up. We keep going and fight. God balances things out, and enlightens us, and gives us a way to face challenges!

The stories in this book represent the different seasons women go through, good and bad times. This book is for women who want to change, to have a better life and be happy. Too many people stay hurt, accuse others, and cause themselves depression and despair. When it comes to the possibility of being healed, they do not hear the simple words of St. Thomas Aquinas: *Si vis*, "If you want to." Consider the words of St. Augustine: *Time Dominum transeutem*, "I am afraid the Lord may pass by." We lose a precious opportunity to change when we do not want to change. Everyone has so many excuses; some of them come from the devil, a cunning enemy. But in reality, those excuses are accusations.

The Church offers many methods for healing, from the Rosary to daily Mass and Confession. Which methods you use is up to you, but you must be consistent and persevere, so you will be able to say with St. Paul, "I have fought the good fight, I have finished the race, I have kept the faith" (2 Tim. 4:7). These are steps for healing:

1. Have a routine, for without routine, we fall into despair.
2. Lift your heart to God all day with invocations.
3. Force yourself to acquire virtues, and you will obtain the essential virtue: interior peace.

Isaiah 43:4 says, "You are precious." God is calling you to be a great saint! I pray that you will be the best!

— Rev. Louis M. Solcia, CRSP, MA, MED

Dare to be
different by doing
what's right!

MOTHER ANGELICA

CHAPTER 1

UNBROKEN

Crystalina Evert

Have you ever felt that you are not enough, that you amount to less than those around you, or that a situation was too much to handle? Did your self-doubt then kick in, and did you start questioning your ability and skills? Have you felt that you do not deserve the love and blessings God has placed before you? Have you thought that you are not smart or pretty enough compared with others? Have you allowed fear to prevent you from moving forward to attain a specific goal? Did you ever ignore that still, small voice nudging you to do or say something; or did you decide to act on it, only to talk yourself out of it?

Unfortunately, I have ignored that still, small voice on many occasions. We are all guilty of giving in to self-doubt and fear because somehow that negative voice seems more powerful than the still, small voice assuring us that we have what it takes.

There was a time in my life when I allowed those doubts and insecurities to control me by living a life of grave sin through my wounds. Those doubts and insecurities slowly dominated me and evolved into fear. I became careless in how I chose to live my life, and I dismissed God's will and His many attempts to reach my heart. Ignoring Him seemed much easier than responding to Him. My pride was an obstacle to His grace as I held on to the false reality that I was "in control." I was swayed by the opinions of others, and I defined myself by my past mistakes and by my upbringing in a dysfunctional family. How many countless years, days, and

3

hours I wasted on the petty things of this world and the people who did not care about me!

I had no understanding of my true purpose and was afraid to surrender to God's plan for my life. My disobedience to His call hindered the work He wanted to do within me. Over time, I became someone I never wanted to be. It is so easy to make excuses, but I've learned that excuses are just lies we tell ourselves. As I look back, taking the "easy road" made my life more difficult in the long run. The struggle grew more intense as the hole I was digging for myself became deeper.

During my high school years, I had no interest in my Catholic Faith and often doubted the existence of God. I spent my time keeping up appearances to protect my family's image. I agreed to go to Confession only to appease my mother so she would allow me the freedom to be with my "friends." But after many reckless weekends of drinking, drugs, and casual sexual encounters, my life spiraled out of control. I felt like trash—utterly worthless. The void in my heart was so big that I grew discouraged and believed it was much too late for me to change.

I didn't know then that God has an assignment, a mission, and a plan for each of us. The problem is that we often ignore it because we are too busy listening to others and living according to the world's ways. We make the mistake of looking outside ourselves for the answers, and we end up going down a rabbit hole that can consume us. Without the firm foundation of faith and God's grace, we will always end up questioning who we are.

Jesus challenges us women of God, young or old, not to be of the world. He tells us in John 15:19, "If you were of the world, the world would love its own: but because you are not of the world, but I chose you out of the world, therefore the world hates you." If Jesus Himself tells us we are not of this world, why do we try to solve our problems with a worldly mindset, leaving Jesus out of our life decisions, as if He doesn't care about them? We end up settling for scraps the world gives us. As a result, we are frustrated, disappointed, and always left in a state of longing. But Jesus wants to give us so much more—more than we can ever imagine!

Every decision we make matters and has some impact on the rest of our lives. When we go against what we know is right, most of us feel it in the depths of our hearts. Think about your own life. Are you dating someone you know you shouldn't be? Are you afraid to embrace a specific vocation because you don't want to miss out on something else or because you fear you will end up like your parents? Maybe you are struggling with an addiction to social media or are viewing immoral entertainment you know you should not be watching. We convince ourselves that our poor choices are not that bad. If we feel the need to justify what we are doing, well, what we are doing is probably not good. I have fallen into this evil trap many times over.

Have I failed in areas of my life at times? Absolutely! But does that determine a life sentence of failure? It depends on whether I give up.

We will always be tempted to give up and dwell on the past. The important thing is to be intentional and honest with ourselves in answering *why*. This small word helps us understand who we are and what we will become. *Why* is not easy to ask. Why did I sexualize my anger when I was younger? Why did I push people away? Why was it hard for me to receive and give love? Why did I struggle with my vocation as a wife and mother? To go deeper and find the answers, I needed to ask these tough questions. But I didn't dive into them on my own. I was able to face my deepest wounds only with Jesus. Frankly, I didn't want to go into those dark places within myself without Him. He gave me the courage, strength, and grace to go into those broken places and deal with the mess I had created for myself. There are some things only Jesus could help me overcome. But I needed to face those hard truths, to own what happened to me, and to heal so that I could move in the direction God wanted me to go.

Since my early twenties, I've had a strong devotion to St. Thérèse of Lisieux. She was a simple cloistered nun who did small things with great, childlike love. During her time on earth, she was considered a nobody in the eyes of the world. However, she was a force to be reckoned with in the spiritual realm. St. Thérèse knew that she was created for more, and she made the decision to sow the seeds of her divine mission. She knew that her real mission would begin when she died. She said: "After my death I will let fall a shower of roses. . . . I will spend my Heaven doing good on earth."[1] For years, I have treasured one of her sayings: "He has never inspired me with any desire and left it unsatisfied"[2] These words have helped me understand that if God asks me to do something, no matter how small the task, it must be significant. In my spiritual journey, I have learned to take this very seriously. Too often, we get stuck in our heads and give in to thinking that what God asks of us does not matter. We are tempted to talk ourselves out of doing what He asks of us and to justify ourselves in doing so. As a result, we grow further away from our hearts, which is exactly where God speaks to us.

I want to share with you the moment that changed the course of my entire life. It was when I heard a brave young man give his testimony about how Jesus healed him from his godless lifestyle. This is when the concept of "starting over" was first introduced

---

[1] St. Thérèse of Lisieux, *Story of a Soul*, epilogue.
[2] Ibid., chap. 7.

to me. It seemed foreign to me at the time. But what struck me was this man's peace, joy, and holy confidence. He seemed so unashamed when he spoke about the bad choices he had made. I completely identified with his past mistakes, which paralleled mine. Yet he was free and not weighed down by the burden of his sin. I tried to think of a day when I wasn't ashamed. The sad truth was that I couldn't think of one.

And so my spiritual journey back to God began at that moment with one simple yes. I knew that if I truly wanted to turn my life around, I needed to start with an honest confession. From there, the graces began to flow, and for the first time in my life, I felt free. What a grace-filled Lazarus moment! With all my heart, I know that if I didn't say yes to Jesus' invitation, I would never have married Jason—that brave young man—and would not have been involved with our important ministry work. If I had said "maybe later," my ten children would never have come into existence, and I wouldn't be sitting here writing this book.

Mother Angelica said, "Everything starts with one person.... I don't care if you're five or one hundred and five; from all eternity, God chose you to be where you are at this time in history to change the world."

What you do now on earth matters and holds heavenly weight. Of course, you have been given the gift of free will in making choices. God the Father will never force Himself on you. But every decision you make will have an eternal effect on the state of your soul. Your yes is everything! Your obedience is vital, and God will give you the grace and courage to face your fears and get through whatever He is asking of you.

Some time ago, a woman wrote to me: "Thank you, Crystalina. I am seventy-five years old and ready to heal. My father sexually abused me until I was eighteen, and I couldn't escape. I carried these wounds and secrets all my life, but now I finally have the courage to start my healing process." I was brought to tears and so happy for this woman who had the courage to face what happened to her fifty-seven years ago. God's mercy is endless!

I'm sure you listened to that small, still voice of the Holy Spirit when you decided to read this book. Nothing is ever a coincidence with God. He has something He wants to say to you, and He invites you to go deeper. No pretending, no excuses.

So here are some questions I'd like you to ask yourself:

- Am I truly the woman God is calling me to be? If not, why not?
- When was the last time I took a sobering look at myself?

Some women choose to live their lives in complete denial. Others avoid and deflect the truth and are driven by their fears. You and I are going to be different. We were created "for such a time as this" (Esther 4:14). We are strong, capable, and worthy of the mission God is calling us to. We need not remain complacent and adopt the falsehood that "this is all there is."

I am an abuse survivor, a woman from a broken family who was almost crushed by the weight of a sinful lifestyle, but the Eternal Father proved His faithfulness to me. He is a God of second chances; I am living proof of that. Look at how He has used me to do His work! Jesus will use you, too, but you must listen to Him and be ready for spiritual battle against the enemies of your soul.

I have in my office a picture that reminds me of this spiritual battle. It is a large photo of St. Thérèse dressed as St. Joan of Arc, wearing armor and holding a sword in her hand. To the right of her is her shield. As I was gazing at this picture the other day, I noticed for the first time a crown of roses next to her shield, hanging on a branch. I believe this foreshadowed the crown of roses she would receive in Heaven and give back to us here on earth.

During her lifetime, this great saint was small and hidden from the world. Today, she is a Doctor of the Church. Some may say, "Well, she was a saint, and I can never attain that level of holiness." Don't sell yourself short or put limits on the importance of your mission. Whatever our state in life, God is calling every one of us to be a saint.

The truth is we are all striving for a crown. James 1:12 tells us, "Blessed is the man who endures trial, for when he has stood the test he will receive the crown of life which God has promised to those who love him." Our striving for this crown need not be arduous. In a letter to her sister Céline, St. Thérèse of Lisieux wrote, "The good God does not need years to accomplish His work of love in a soul; one ray from His Heart can, in an instant, make His flower bloom for eternity."

Have you had enough of being consumed by the trappings of the world? Are you willing to detach from your old ways and take on the new? What virtues would you like to trade for the vices you struggle with? Do you believe, without a shadow of a doubt, that you were created for much more? Do you believe God can transform your life and make you whole again?

My invitation to you now is this: Face it! Own it! Heal it! Make the decision to abandon yourself to God's will. Trust Him! He will give you what you need to take the next step. Remember, it's never too late to start over. It doesn't matter who you are, where you've been, or what you've done. All that matters now is where you go from here!

The Spirit gave us
His gifts so we would
be clothed with the
jewels of virtue, the
gold of love, the
emeralds of hope,
and the brilliant
diamonds of faith.
Let us not be content
with the Scotch tape
and the aluminum
foil of this world.

MOTHER ANGELICA

CHAPTER 2

REGRET, REMORSE, AND SORROW

Mother Angelica

Whenever you do anything wrong in your life, the first thing you usually do is regret it. Now, there are times after we regret something that we have remorse, and this remorse can be deadly. There are other times when we have a sorrow in our hearts, and this sorrow can be deadly, or it can be fruitful. All of these can be stepping-stones to great virtue and the fruits of the Spirit, or they can lead us all the way down into despair.

Now, I want to look at something from the Gospel that gives us an excellent example of how two people handle basically the same sin. First we have Peter in the Garden of Gethsemane. When the soldiers seized Jesus, Peter tried to defend Him. He took out his sword and cut off the ear of the high priest's slave, and our Lord healed that ear.

Well, by that time, Peter had become very frightened, and he ran. And running like that is usually the beginning of something—a deep or grievous sin. Sometimes we do things because we're afraid, and we run, and then, in that effort, fear makes us fall.

Next, we see Peter in the high priest's courtyard. The servants had lit a fire, and Peter sat down among them. That was his first mistake. Here, we're going to see the role of regret, remorse, sorrow, and forgiveness, which we'll come to later. We're also going to see how we put ourselves in occasions of sin.

See, we always think we can handle things. Well, Peter teaches us a tremendous lesson about human nature. You and I have done the same thing Peter did. There's no way you can say, "Well, I would never do that." Yeah, you've done it; I've done it.

The Gospel says, "He was sitting there by the blaze, and a servant girl saw him and peered at him." You know why it says she peered at him? You know what that means? "Peer" means to kind of examine somebody from his feet to his head. Well, while the servant girl's eyes were going up and coming down again, Peter was scared to death.

Now, if he had been smart, he would have said, "Excuse me, my mother-in-law's calling me" or "Somebody needs me" or "I have an appointment" and would have gotten out of there. But no, he just sat there. And the servant girl said, "This person has been with Him!"

And Peter denied it. He said, "I don't know Him." Wow! See, fear makes you do things that you don't want to do and that you know you shouldn't do.

And then somebody else came along and looked Peter up and down and, maybe stroking his beard a bit, said, "Hmm, you are one of them." And Peter said, "I'm not, my friend." So he was calling somebody he never saw in his life a friend.

The next incident happened "an hour later." Now, that is a long time. Don't you think you'd have gotten out of a situation like that? Don't you think that, by that time, you'd have said, "I've gotta get out of here! I'm going to fall flat on my face!"

But haven't you been in a situation where you knew you should get out of a place before you fell flat? And what did you do? You stayed another hour. That's exactly what Peter did.

Another man came along and said, "This man was certainly with Him. Why, he's a Galilean. His speech betrays him." "My friend, I do not know what you're talking about." Now, without any excuses, Peter lied.

Peter lied three times. He denied that he knew Jesus. The lie was a denial.

Now, this is what's so heartrending. "While he was speaking, the cock crowed, and the Lord passed by." Can you imagine that? There was Peter among his "friends," and he was swearing and was acting like them, and fear kind of took hold of him. Then Jesus passed by and looked at Peter. He looked at him with such a loving, compassionate, forgiving love. "He looked straight at Peter, and Peter remembered what the Lord said." And what did the Lord say? Well, St. Luke says that shortly before this happened, the Lord had said, "Simon, Simon, Satan, you must know, has got his wish to sift you all like wheat. But I have prayed for you, Simon, that your faith may not fail, and once you have recovered, you, in turn, must strengthen your brothers."

And Peter had replied, "Nah! Not me. I'm ready to go to prison with You." And our Lord said, "Peter, before the crock crows today, you will have denied me three times."

Now, you see the difference between the heart and the love of Jesus, the compassion of Jesus, and ours. In that look of Jesus, there was no condemnation. It was a look of tremendous, compassionate love, and that brought about in Peter great sorrow, because the Gospel says, "He went out and wept bitterly."

Now, we're going to look at the difference between Peter and Judas. Peter had deep sorrow. He admitted his sin. Judas became first regretful and then turned to remorse, and that is why he committed suicide; he hanged himself.

When I am regretful, it is a kind of sorrow. But in this case, I am sorry not because I offended someone but because I did something wrong. So I regret what I did. I regret and you regret many things, but we regret not because something turned out bad but because we were stupid enough to make it turn out bad! "If I hadn't done that, this wouldn't have happened." That's regret.

Now, Peter could have said the same thing. He could have said, "Why did I stay in that stupid circle, warming myself? I should have gotten out of there after the first question." He didn't have regret. He wept bitterly because he was sorrowful. He admitted his sin.

Sometimes when we regret, our admission leads to remorse. What is remorse? It is a lack of hope.

Say I did something, and I regret it, meaning, "I'm sorry. That was a stupid act." Regret came with the sorrow, the right kind. But what if I begin to live in this regret and it never leaves my mind? What if it doesn't turn to tearful sorrow—sorrow not because I have done something wrong but because I have offended the all-holy God or a dear friend or the community, or I have offended the nation by scandal. See, the whole thing comes down not so much to what I did but what I did to other people.

Now, remorse is an aspect of regret that focuses on self. Regret says, "I was so stupid! I sold this business, and two weeks later, its value increased a millionfold. What a dummy I am!" But what if I were to say, "I made a mistake here, but maybe those millions wouldn't have been good for me. Lord, help me to be discerning in the future. But I thank You because maybe those millions of dollars would have made me go astray."

If I didn't say that—and believe me, nobody has offered me a million dollars, so don't get excited—what would I say? I would concentrate on regret: I missed an opportunity. I missed an investment. Or I had this opportunity to expose my singing talent or my musical talents, and I could have won that prize, and I didn't win that prize, and why didn't I win it? And how come I didn't discern? And that pattern goes on and on and on and on. It becomes a broken record. At some point, remorse comes in. I begin to lie in my own mud puddle.

Our human nature tends toward regret and remorse. It takes a spiritual nature to become sorrowful and repentant. Neither regret nor remorse brings repentance; both bring only a deep sorrow over being wrong about something, making the wrong decision, being stupid, making a mistake; and that sorrow closes you in like a turtle. You don't ask for forgiveness because you think, "How can I be forgiven? How can anybody be forgiven after such a stupid mistake?" And that's why Judas hanged himself and why Peter was sorrowful. Judas regretted. He went to the temple, and he threw the thirty pieces of silver on the floor, and he said, "I have betrayed an innocent man." The chief priests and the elders said, "Hey, that's your problem. What do we have to do with that?"

Talk about hypocrisy and lies! The chief priests and the elders were the ones who got Judas into that situation: they're the ones who asked him to find Jesus, who asked him to betray Jesus, who offered him the thirty pieces of silver. Then they had the audacity to try to remove themselves from their responsibility and say, "Look, we can't touch that money. It's unclean! Let's buy a field up here and bury all the poor people, all the indigents, all the lepers."

Sorrow and regret look alike, but they're different. Judas showed regret: "I have betrayed an innocent man." He knew. He regretted an action, and then he became remorseful. He became centered on himself because he wouldn't have been able to face Jesus. He wouldn't have been able to face the apostles. He couldn't get away from his miserable self.

But Peter wept bitterly and was repentant. "I'm sorry, Lord. I should have listened to You, but I didn't." And we know that Peter had that sorrow because of an incident by the Sea of Tiberias, where he and some others had been fishing. The risen Jesus appeared to them and said to Peter, "Do you love me more than these [others]?" Peter had once said, "Look, all these are going to betray You—not me," which meant that he loved Him more than the others. But now Peter got a little uneasy. See, he was catching on, and he said, "Yes, I love You." No more bravado. Sorrow made him dependent on God. He knew he could no longer make those foolhardy statements.

And our Lord said, "Well, feed my sheep." And He said, "Peter, do you love me more than these?"

"Lord, You know I love You."

"Feed My lambs. Peter, do you love me more than these?"

"Lord!" By this time, Peter's sorrow and dependence on God were getting kind of desperate, and he said, "Lord, You know all things. You know I love You."

A grace was offered both to Judas and to Peter. Peter was impulsive and impetuous. He never lost faith in Jesus. "Lord," he had said, "Thou art the Christ, the Son of the Most High God." And Jesus said, "Men, flesh, had not revealed this to you, but my Father in heaven has revealed this to you." So Peter never lost faith or trust in Jesus, even after such a terrible sin. He could ask for forgiveness and receive forgiveness.

Judas did not ask. He took his own life into his hands. He hanged himself, which showed despair and remorse. Judas went into himself. He didn't have much faith in Jesus, or he would never have denied Him. But Scripture said he was a liar and a thief (see John 12:6). He wasn't interested in the poor, only in himself.

Peter was impetuous; he made a mistake, but he loved Jesus. Well, real sorrow that comes from having offended someone, not from what you particularly did, brings repentance—meaning, "I'm very sorry, Lord."

Repentance doesn't mean only sorrow. You can be sorry for everything and never say, "Please forgive me." Judas never asked for forgiveness. He was regretful about an act; he became remorseful, and he killed himself. Peter was sorrowful; he admitted his sin. He said, "I'm sorry, Lord." He wept bitterly, and he became dependent—no longer independent, no longer self-oriented, no longer self-sufficient. He knew. "Lord, You know I love You." He never lost faith or trust.

Now, that's the negative of everything. When we talk about the gifts of the Spirit, we're going to see something different.[3]

When we are conscious of our faults and weaknesses—and no matter how grievous they may be, we may have committed all seven capital sins—it's very possible that we each have just one that we call a predominant fault, the one that makes us fall the most. Judas and Peter fell under their predominant faults. And one of Peter's faults was that he was impetuous, but so was Judas. Judas waited three years for Jesus to be the kind of Messiah he wanted, and he had had it! No more! So both Peter and Judas were impetuous; both were tired of something; both were afraid. But their reactions were totally different.

The Holy Spirit grants us the gift to forgive and accept both repentance and sorrow. Have you ever humbled yourself enough to say to someone, "I'm sorry; I didn't mean to do that" and found that the person wouldn't forgive you? "Look, just get out of my sight. I don't want to see you anymore." There is nothing worse. So I have to be able to forgive. I have to be able to accept somebody else's repentance. If you say to me, "I'm sorry," I have to be able to accept that and say, "It's okay. Let's go on from here. Let's just forget whatever happened." That's a gift of the Holy Spirit. It's the gift to forgive and to accept the repentance of my neighbor.

Now, I must keep myself from going into remorse. Regret means I'm sorry I did something; it's a beginning, but if I don't get myself out of it, then I go into remorse. A great gift of the Holy Spirit

---

[3] In this chapter, Mother Angelica discusses gifts of the Holy Spirit other than the traditional seven. —Ed.

that we need to ask for is endurance. I need endurance to be able to put up with myself and the faults of my neighbors. How many people get disgusted with others' faults? That disgust might even lead them to leave their families or to get a divorce. Some people get so upset over their own faults and weaknesses that they go into despair.

I need endurance. I need perseverance. I need to know that I am a frail, weak human being. And because I am frail and weak, I have a tendency to do what Peter did, even maybe what Judas did. But if I have other gifts of the Spirit, love and hope, these will make me repentant and make me run to Jesus. Regret and remorse would make me run away from Jesus.

See, repentance makes you run to, and regret and remorse make you run from. And that's the essence of Hell. All the people in Hell have regret and remorse but have no sorrow, no repentance. If the Lord God Himself came down and said, "Will you repent? Will you love me as Lord of all in my Incarnation?" they would say, "No!" You see, there's no repentance; there's no admission; there's no love and no hope. In Hell, there is no hope. In Judas, there was no hope. In Peter, there *was* hope. In Judas, no faith. In Peter, there *was* faith. There was a lot of weakness in Peter, but his faith didn't fail. He denied Jesus out of fear. And one look from Jesus, one thought of Jesus, changed the whole picture.

One of the great fruits of the Spirit is joy. After you have sinned and said you're sorry and accepted Jesus' forgiveness, one of the greatest things you can do for Him, one of the greatest ways you can glorify Him, is to have joy. No remorse. Remorse takes away joy. If I have regret without sorrow, then I'll go to remorse, because sorrow is a heart thing and regret is a head thing.

Now, once you ask forgiveness, you must still accept the circumstances; things don't change. Your son is sixteen years old, and he just got his driver's license, and you just bought a brand-new car, and he wrapped it around a tree. Now, he can say he's sorry. Does it straighten out the car? Does he look at that car, one big piece of junk now, and say, "I'm sorry," and some magic thing happens? No! He's got to make restitution. He may get himself a job and have to work for three years to pay you back. He just can't walk away and say, "Well, I'm sorry about that, Dad. Let the insurance cover it." How would you feel if he said that?

So, when I ask for forgiveness, I have to accept the responsibility for my mistake. Peter accepted the responsibility for his mistake! I don't think he ever forgot that he denied the Lord, but it was always a source of joy to him because he was the recipient of tremendous love, fantastic hope, and joy!

The Eternal Father sent Jesus to make restitution for us. Jesus died once for all. Why? For our sins. But I still have to make reparation and accept the consequences of my mistakes. But you see, the gifts of the Holy Spirit, love and hope, make me know I can depend on the Lord's strength, forgiveness, and mercy, as long as I say, "I'm sorry." But it takes the gift of the Holy Spirit to do that.

I need also peace. Sorrow that comes from my heart, that makes me say to God or my neighbor, "I'm sorry," brings me peace. Those of you who are Catholic and have gone to Confession with quite a load have experienced a joy that no other thing would give you. There is something about hearing, "I absolve you from all your sins." So I know for sure I am forgiven.

Then the Spirit comes along with hope and joy and peace. Look at St. Paul. He ran after Christians. We don't always look at that. He dragged them into prison—women, children, and men—dragged them out of their homes, dragged them from places where they were hiding, and put them in jail, had them flogged, perhaps took away their possessions. That's pretty tough stuff. Did he ever forget it? No. Was he regretful? No. He said, "Even though I was a persecutor of the Church of Christ, even though I did all of these terrible things, the Lord has forgiven me," and that gave him hope, joy, and peace. He did not regret what he did because he did it with sincerity as a faithful Jew, a Pharisee.

Now, if I commit a grievous sin, and I know ahead of time that it's a grievous sin, I may regret what I did, but that regret must lead to repentance. It must lead to repentance because repentance and sorrow are also gifts of the Spirit. I need grace from God.

Regret can be the beginning of something great or the beginning of something evil. It could be the beginning of a total dependence on God; it could be the beginning of being forgiven and experiencing His love, His mercy, and His joy; or it could be the beginning of guilt, remorse, and despair. There is a point in regret—meaning, "I'm sorry I did this"—that either turns inward or upward. At that point—this is what you need to be careful about—where is your regret? Where is your sorrow then? Does it lead to love and joy and peace and compassion for your neighbor? If you have failed miserably, how can you possibly be impatient with your neighbor? Isn't that what the Lord said? "Take the beam out of your own eye" (see Matt. 7:5).

Some people never go through the regret stage because they're so filled with faith and hope. And if they fall out of weakness or whatever, they turn immediately to God. There's no regret necessary. They have an inner awareness. If you love someone deeply, you don't have to analyze it; you know right away when you have hurt that person. You see it in the person's face, and you say, "Why did I say that? I'm going to bite my tongue next time." And you didn't mean it when it was coming out either, but you knew immediately that it hurt somebody.

I want you to imagine here a great, big mud puddle. And three people are going to go past it. Here comes an evil man, one who enjoys evil, and he slips in the mud puddle, and he loves it! He keeps putting mud all over himself, and he just sits there, and he loves that mud puddle. That's an evil person who loves evil, loves darkness, loves sin.

A good person comes, and he falls into the mud puddle, and he gets up. He sits there a little bit, though. He says, "Oh, why did I come this way? Somebody told me this mud puddle was here. Why did I do it?" He keeps sitting there. "This is terrible. I'm wasting all this time." He just keeps sitting there. "I don't know why I did this. It's just so stupid of me to do this after I've been warned. You'd think I'd have enough sense to …" Still sitting there! Finally, he says, "Well, I'd better get up. This is ridiculous, my sitting here." So he gets out of the mud puddle, and he starts walking around, and sometimes he says, "Oh, look at me, I'm all covered with mud. What's my wife going to say when I get home? What are the people around me going to say? Lord, what am I going to do?" Now, he's up, isn't he? He's out of the mud puddle. He's sorry he got in that mud puddle. But he says, "Oh my, what am I going to do?"

Now, here comes a saintly person we could call a good Christian—all good Christians are saints. And he comes along, and down he goes. And he says, "Woo!" and gets up like that. He says, "Sorry, Lord. I'll watch it next time. Please forgive me." He goes on and never thinks of his dirty clothes, never thinks of what people are going say—nothing at all. He just keeps praising the Lord. He says, "Lord, I know You love me, and Your love is always faithful."

We're like little bitty drops in the ocean. And that's what we need to understand. If you have sinned or you just can't accept your weaknesses, then be repentant, ask for forgiveness, and say, "Jesus, I love You with my whole heart." Let the Spirit fill you with love and peace and joy, and be a witness to His forgiving, merciful love. God bless you.

Faith is one foot on
the ground, one
foot in the air, and
a queasy feeling
in the stomach.

MOTHER ANGELICA

CHAPTER 3

"SURRENDER" IS NOT A FOUR-LETTER WORD

Teresa Tomeo

I am the vine, you are the branches.
He who abides in me, and I in him, he
it is that bears much fruit, for apart
from me you can do nothing.

JOHN 15:5

There I was, all alone and at the foot of the crucifix that was hanging on our bedroom wall. The tears just kept flowing. From my vantage point, or that of anyone peeking through the curtains, the image of a strong, independent woman—a successful broadcast journalist with shelves filled with awards and countless photos of worldly accomplishments—was shattered. This well-known local media personality had been knocked off her high horse. The person surrounded by a pile of well-used tissues, her face smudged with mascara, did not resemble the reporter who had graced the TV screens of millions of residents in southeastern Michigan. Looking back now, I realize that, from God's point of view, this scene was a thing of beauty, as I had finally said, "Jesus, take the wheel."

It was the first time, even after returning to the Catholic Church and making a commitment to Christ a few months earlier, that I *completely* surrendered my life, entrusting my entire will to His.

Because of His enormous love for me, for you, and for every person on His green earth, God regards complete brokenness, along with a real desire to begin again, as a work of precious art—a scene fit for the Vatican Museums, the Uffizi Gallery in Florence, or New York's Metropolitan Museum of Art. I think you get the picture, pun intended.

Now, do not get me wrong. It is not as if I had this huge one-and-done awakening. The clouds did not suddenly disappear and leave the sun shining brightly in their place. Dropping to my knees in the privacy of my home that early spring morning three decades ago was truly an act of sheer desperation. My tireless efforts to get things right with God, with the world, and with my career, or what was left of it—surprise, surprise!—were not working. So as a final attempt to find answers, I *totally* gave in to God. If my stubbornness in refusing to let go and "let God" lingered months after a recent and pivotal journey back to the Catholic Church, how much more difficult is it for our brothers and sisters who are still fallen away? What about those referred to as the "nones," men and women who were raised in Christian homes but no longer identify with any religion or church? How difficult is it for them to find their way home? What about the countless who are enduring great suffering and wondering where God is in the midst of their pain?

There are answers to these crucial questions, but we must know, love, and trust the One Who has the answers before we can accept them and move toward achieving God's special plans for each of us. And therein lies the rub. The path to that point of acceptance and relinquishing of the will is different for each of us.

There is no better place on earth for a woman than to be in relationship with Jesus in the Catholic Church. And since faith is a journey, the first step on our journey—if true happiness and fulfillment are our goals—is that ultimate act of surrendering heart, soul, mind, and strength (Luke 10:27; Matt. 22:37; Mark 12:30).

Unfortunately, the idea of surrender in today's world often conjures up frightening images. The Wicked Witch of the West, made famous by the classic children's film *The Wizard of Oz*, comes to mind. Who can forget the look of absolute terror on Dorothy's face as she watched the witch fly across the sky, writing in big black letters "Surrender, Dorothy"? To Dorothy, the word "surrender" represented death. The witch was determined to get those ruby slippers and would stop at nothing; she even threatened to take the lives of Dorothy, her friends, and Toto, too, if Dorothy did not give in.

Likewise, in numerous war movies and science fiction films, surrendering is something that someone does when he is trapped or captured, when all hope is lost. Hollywood's idea of surrender is almost always associated with giving in to the bad guy, whether a witch, a grotesque creature, crooked cops, or anyone else who does not have the good guy's best interests at heart.

But it's not just Hollywood that gives us a negative impression of surrender. Our culture in general reminds us practically around the clock—given our level of media exposure and consumption—that we are the captains of our own vessels. Being truly free means giving in to whatever we want to do, with whomever we choose and whenever and however we choose. Our personal desires and needs are steering the ship. Even when, as was the case with me, God and the Church serve as occasional first mates, offering some guidance or direction, at the end of the day, me, myself, and I are in charge. "We've got this, thank you." If we turn over the controls, we're convinced we will be on the losing end of life. Thinking about surrender can give us an instant and severe case of FOMO—*fear of missing out.* End of story. So we keep doing what we want to do, only—as I discovered—to find ourselves shipwrecked with no rescue vessel or cavalry on the horizon.

From the Christian perspective, as Pope Francis explained in his October 20, 2021, General Audience message, surrendering to God is the ultimate victory rather than a humiliating loss. It's the beginning rather than the end of our story:

> Freedom is very different from license; it is not found in giving in to our own selfish desires, but instead leads us to serve others. True freedom is fully expressed in love.

And this, as the pope reminds us, is the great paradox of the Gospel message.

> We are freed by serving, we find ourselves fully to the extent that we give ourselves; we possess life if we lose it.

A great paradox indeed. The pope is reiterating the words of Jesus, who said that, in order to gain our life, we must lose it.

> For whoever would save his life will lose it, and whoever loses his life for my sake will find it. (Matt. 16:25)

I remember when I enrolled in my first Bible study and came across these seemingly contradictory verses. I spent a lot of time scratching my head, trying to figure out what they meant and how they applied to my life. The more I studied, prayed, and grew in my relationship with Jesus, the more these words began to make sense. When we give our lives over to God in that ultimate act of surrender, God gives us a new life in return.

As St. Paul points out in 2 Corinthians 5:17, "If any one is in Christ, he is a new creation; the old has passed away, behold, the new has come."

Despite the progress I thought I was making before that desperate moment at the foot of the crucifix, I came to realize that I was still a lot like Dorothy. Surrendering still represented death to me—death, that is, to the goals I had at the time. God was beginning slowly to unveil an entirely different plan for my life, and up to that point, I was not ready to discover what that plan might be, as I was convinced that my plan was so much better (like Dorothy's plan to live anywhere but in Kansas). I thought that God just needed to help me get my plan done and wrap it in a nice big bow.

Prior to what would be my first of many "come-to-Jesus moments," I had been working in the secular media as a news anchor for almost fifteen years. I was the "it" girl in local TV news in my hometown of metropolitan Detroit. However, in the news business, the management often changes on-air personalities as quickly as one changes a tie or undergarments. And that's what happened to me. Despite my success, I took a huge leap downward overnight. One moment, I was presenting the lead story on the evening news. The next day, I was standing in the unemployment line. My contract was about to expire, and the management, due to poor ratings, decided it was time to shake things up. Several co-workers were also let go over several weeks. Everyone in the news business realizes how volatile a profession journalism can be. But despite the job insecurity, somehow you still never expect to be the one on the chopping block.

As jolting as it was, the sudden dismissal would eventually end up being both the worst thing and the best thing that ever happened to me. Given how I let my career dominate my life and practically ruin my marriage, the six months off the job gave my husband and me the necessary time to refocus on our relationship. About a year before my dismissal, as God would have it, my husband received what we now realize was nothing short of a miraculous invitation to a men's Bible study. I don't know which was more miraculous: the fact that the invitation came from a media colleague at a Detroit Pistons basketball game, of all places, or the fact that my husband said yes on the spot. We were at that game with some co-workers of mine, one of whom was a local radio producer who happened to be a devout Christian. My husband, Dom, is an engineer who, as he likes to say, has the paralysis of overanalysis. But that Scripture program changed his life. It started him on the fast track toward a renewed relationship with Jesus and led him, years later, to discern a calling to the diaconate. He was ordained a deacon in October 2012. The Scripture program also prepared him for the challenges of dealing with a wife who was dazed, confused, and pretty darn angry over her job situation and over life in general.

Thanks be to God, about the time I was let go, the same Bible study leaders were offering a class for couples. Since I didn't have much else to do with my time, I agreed to take the course with my husband. I slowly began my way home, and bit by bit, Dom and I began to put the pieces of our shattered marriage back together. Despite my interior struggles, as a cradle Catholic I knew deep down that I had put my faith and my marriage on the back burner to forge ahead professionally. "Career first" was drilled into my head in journalism school, as it was for most women attending college in the late seventies and early eighties. We are women; hear us roar. Take no prisoners, and let nothing and no one get in the way. Well, how did that work out for me and for so many others? It almost cost me everything—not only my marriage but, even more important, my soul.

Despite the learning process that was occurring with my faith and the healing taking place in my marriage, I still felt adrift. I just couldn't understand why God wasn't putting me back on the air, especially after I was once again taking Him and the sacrament of Marriage seriously. No matter how hard I tried, I was unable to find work. And that brings us back to that fateful moment under the crucifix. After months of pounding the pavement, with nothing to show for it, I begged God to show me what *He* wanted. I remember asking Him from the depths of my heart, *"What do You want me to do?"* And that was the key that opened the door to a new relationship with God and His Church and, to my surprise, to a new type of career in an entirely different type of media.

It's so important to remember that our Lord is a gentleman. He is always waiting for us with open arms, but the decision must be ours. He will never take away our free will; otherwise we would be like puppets on a string. In Revelation 3:20, we read that Jesus is at the door, waiting for us to open it.

> Behold, I stand at the door and knock; if any one hears my voice and opens the door, I will come in to him and eat with him, and he with me.

The famous painting *The Light of the World* captures this wonderful verse. The artist, William Holman Hunt, depicts Jesus knocking on a large door. But look closely: there is no doorknob. The knobless door is meant to represent the importance of being open to Christ's coming into our lives and our hearts. The artist also indicated that the painting is meant to represent our obstinance in refusing to allow God to be the Lord of our lives.

My favorite saint is the first female to be declared a Doctor of the Church, Teresa of Ávila. She is noted for her feisty personality, her sense of humor, and most of all, her profound mystical writings and her incredible down-to-earth love of Jesus. Many Catholics are familiar with the following words of wisdom from St. Teresa, commonly referred to as "Let Nothing Disturb You":

> Let nothing disturb you,
> Nothing frighten you.
> All things are passing.
> God never changes.
> Patience obtains all things.
> Nothing is wanting in him who possesses God.
> God alone suffices.

This is one of my favorite prayers as well. However, a few years ago when I was leading a pilgrimage to Ávila, Spain, I came across another prayer of this great teacher, and it packs an even more powerful punch. It speaks directly to the importance of repeatedly surrendering our will over to God, regardless of our circumstances. The first time I read this prayer, titled "In the Hands of God," sometimes referred to as "St. Teresa's Love Song," it brought me right back to that pivotal moment in my life at the foot of the crucifix. The complete version is long but worth the read, and it is a must for times when we struggle with trusting in God, especially when we hit bumps in the road.

Read this slowly, and as you linger over the words of this incredible witness, ask St. Teresa and her Spouse, Jesus, to give you the strength to trust totally in *His* plan for you, whatever that might be. Think about the humility of God. If the Ruler of the universe, the King of Kings, can humble Himself to come into the world as a helpless child and then suffer an excruciating and, yes, humiliating death, who are we not to trust in His love and His plan for us? How could anyone Who loves us that much not want anything but the best for us? Keep the question "What do You want of me?" always foremost in your mind and heart. Reflect also on the word "surrender," and ask God to show you the areas of your life that still need surrendering.

> I am Yours and born of You,
> What do You want of me?
> Majestic Sovereign,
> Unending wisdom,
> Kindness pleasing to my soul;
> God sublime, one Being Good,
> Behold this one so vile.
> Singing of her love to You:
> What do You want of me?
>
> Yours, You made me,
> Yours, You saved me,
> Yours, You called me,
> Yours, You awaited me,
> Yours, I did not stray.
> What do You want of me?
>
> Good Lord, what do You want of me?
> What is this wretch to do?
> What work is this,
> This sinful slave, to do?
> Look at me, Sweet Love,
> Sweet Love, look at me,
> What do You want of me?
>
> In Your hand
> I place my heart,
> Body, life, and soul,
> Deep feelings and affections mine,
> Spouse—Redeemer sweet,

Myself offered now to You,
What do You want of me?

Give me death, give me life,
Health or sickness,
Honor or shame,
War or swelling peace,
Weakness or full strength,
Yes, to these I say,
What do You want of me?

Give me wealth or want,
Delight or distress,
Happiness or gloominess,
Heaven or Hell,
Sweet life, sun unveiled,
To You I give all.
What do You want of me?

Give me, if You will, prayer;
Or let me know dryness,
And abundance of devotion,
Or if not, then barrenness.
In You alone, Sovereign Majesty,
I find my peace,
What do You want of me?

Give me, then, wisdom,
Or for love, ignorance,
Years of abundance,
Or hunger and famine.
Darkness or sunlight,
Move me here or there:

What do You want of me?

If You want me to rest,
I desire it for love;
If to labor,
I will die working:
Sweet Love, say
Where, how, and when.
What do You want of me?

Calvary or Tabor give me,
Desert or fruitful land;
As Job in suffering
Or John at Your breast;
Barren or fruited vine,
Whatever be Your will:
What do You want of me?

Be I Joseph chained
Or as Egypt's governor,
David pained
Or exalted high,
Jonas drowned,
Or Jonas freed:
What do You want of me?

Silent or speaking,
Fruit-bearing or barren,
My wounds shown by the Law,
Rejoicing in the tender Gospel;
Sorrowing or exulting,
You alone live in me:
What do You want of me?

Yours I am, for You I was born:
What do You want of me?

My "come-to-Jesus," or surrender, moment at the foot of the crucifix, as I mentioned, would be one of many. We must renew our commitment to Christ daily. Thinking about that experience, I can just see and hear the Lord saying, "Okay, now we're getting somewhere. Now I can begin the work I have planned for you."

And that, dear sister, was exactly what happened—but very slowly. The Lord did answer my prayer. At that time, I desired strongly to be back on the air. The Lord would allow me another six years in the secular media. But a funny thing happened during my last stint as a news reporter. My faith was changing me, and I was beginning to feel like a fish out of water. Newsrooms had been a part of my life since my first days of college. They were a second home to me. But the more I fell in love with Jesus, the more my desires changed. I began to look around and notice the ugliness of the news business. The "if it bleeds, it leads" sensational mentality had taken over, and a strong bias against Christian beliefs and morals was becoming more and more prevalent. I no longer felt that my gifts as a communicator were being used properly. I did not know what was on the horizon, but I knew enough by then to trust God, and in the year 2000, thanks to His love, along with the great love and support of my husband, I walked away from the news business.

Oh, I was a little shaky at first. But then I experienced a real peace in trusting that God would lead me exactly where He wanted me to be. Maybe this explains why my absolute favorite verse is John 15:5.

I am the vine, you are the branches. He who abides in me, and I in him, he it is that bears much fruit, for apart from me you can do nothing

I knew what it was like to live without God. I learned my lessons about the "nothingness" of worldly success. There was no way I was going to let go of the vine. I just needed to keep clinging and surrendering as one of His bendable branches and see what type of fruit He would bring forth.

And bring forth fruit He did. Little by little, step by step, I found myself back on both radio and TV through Ave Maria Radio and EWTN. God has also granted me the privilege of serving Him as a motivational speaker, an author, and a retreat and pilgrimage leader. There have been many ups and downs and challenges along the way. All of us struggle and suffer from time to time, as we live in a fallen world. But God uses everything we go through if we allow Him to do so.

Perhaps you are puzzled as to why God has not answered your prayers for your children to come back to the Church or for a loved one struggling with an illness. You might be in ministry and praying for opportunities to spread the Gospel. Your prayer might be as basic as needing a better-paying job to keep up with the needs of a growing family. For all these needs, surrender and trust are key.

But sometimes, quite frankly, given all that the Church has faced in recent years, a lack of trust, suspicion, or both can prevent us from going further along the path of faith. The sex-abuse crisis has had a devastating impact not only on its many victims but on all Catholics. I am sure I am not the only one who has been asked why someone would still take the Catholic Church seriously, given all the ugly and shocking headlines. Plenty of criticism is also hurled at organized religion in general, given the crisis of abuse and corruption in other churches.

Not to minimize the concerns over this and other issues, but St. Paul tells us in Romans 3:23 that "all have sinned and fall short of the glory of God." Bishops, priests, deacons, nuns, ministry leaders, and even popes are human. They fall short and sin, as do we. Judas betrayed Jesus, and all the disciples except John abandoned Him when He needed them most. And while the world points a finger at Christians, it often forgets that the same scandals are occurring in secular society, including the public schools, college sports, professional sports, Hollywood, and the news media, to name a few examples. A very long list of saints, including Teresa of Ávila, Catherine of Siena, Hildegard, John Vianney, and, more recently, Pio of Pietrelcina (Padre Pio), faced persecution and challenges from corrupt members of the hierarchy. That persecution did not weaken the faith of those saints. Their struggles made them more determined to spread the Gospel. They understood, as should we, that sinful human beings do not minimize or take away from the saving grace of Christ and His Church.

This does not mean we should shrug our shoulders at the end of the day and just move on. We need to pray for our leadership and encourage them to continue addressing the problems. Systems are now in place to report abuse, and we all have a responsibility. Given everything that has occurred, we should also have a higher level of sensitivity and awareness. Focusing on or being consumed by the problems helps no one and only weakens the faith community through bitterness and anger. Don't let the sins of others keep you from embracing Jesus and the Church, as there is so much to gain—most importantly, salvation. If you're struggling with this, take it to the Lord in prayer or speak with someone in the Church whom you trust. And remember, God is weeping even more than you and I over the sins committed.

God knows what we need before we ask. However, He wants us to keep Him close so we do not lose focus. Several years ago, a good friend of mine lost almost everything after her husband died. She thought he had been taking care of the finances, only to realize that was not the case. She was one step away from quite literally being homeless and being forced to move in with her son. While praying amid her financial struggles, she told God that despite the daunting circumstances, she knew Him well enough to know that if He brought her to it, He would see her through it. And He did so by answering that prayer with a high-paying job. The bills did not disappear, but she still had a roof over her head and eventually a steady income to help her get back on track.

With surrendering comes spiritual growth and strength. For a long time, I kept putting God in a box. I thought the best plan for me was to live out my days at a local station covering breaking news, but God had bigger and better ideas that would serve Him and His Church. All our challenges are lessons if we look closely. How many of us are encouraged by real-life success stories? Whether we read about a famous athlete who had to overcome tremendous physical or emotional challenges or about an inventor who eventually achieved great success even though no one believed in him, we are inspired by people's ability to overcome whatever life throws at them. But somehow in our own lives, as well as in our relationships with God, we want to fast-forward past the hard work and the pain. But everything we go through — the good, the bad, and the ugly — can be used for the good.

> We know that in everything God works for good with those who love him, who are called according to his purpose. (Rom. 8:28)

All the experience I gained in the news business — God took it and used it for the development of a Catholic media ministry dedicated to spreading the Faith. The struggles my husband and I experienced are now being used to help other married couples in need. Our sufferings can be used to make a difference.

You are probably familiar with the old saying "to know me is to love me." Getting to know God is an act of love we do daily. Think about your spouse or closest friends. You know them and love them because you have invested and continue to invest much time and effort in those relationships. You visit with them, chat with them, text them, and e-mail them, taking advantage of all sorts of ways to communicate and grow closer to them. They are a major part of your life. The more time you spend with God and the saints, the more you will grow in your knowledge of and love for them. And we can communicate with God anytime anywhere; no cell phone or laptop or any other electronic device is required. We have direct access to the Great I Am 24/7. We communicate with God in a variety of ways, including the following:

1. Greeting the Lord each morning for that daily "surrender" with the words of St. Teresa of Ávila: "I am Yours; I am made for You. What do You want of me?"

2. Frequent reception of the sacraments, such as:
   - attending weekly Mass to fulfill our Sunday obligation
   - taking advantage of daily Mass, if possible
   - receiving the sacrament of Reconciliation once a month

3. Eucharistic adoration (Ponder the fact that the King of the universe, present in the Blessed Sacrament, is waiting to spend some real quality time with you and me. No appointment necessary. Try doing that with the CEO of a major corporation. Security would haul you away in an instant. But the Lord of Lords has an open-door policy.)

4. Scripture reading, including:
   - Praying with the daily Mass readings through a Catholic devotional, such as *Magnificat* (www.

magnificat.net) or *The Word among Us* (www.
wau.org).

&bo; Enrolling in a Catholic Bible study online or
in your parish.

There is no need to wait until a crisis occurs in your life, as it
did in mine. Yes, God is there for us around the clock. And He
can and does exchange beauty for ashes (see Isa. 61:3). But the
crisis in my life, for example, could have been avoided had I not
lost touch with Jesus.

Getting back to our sister Dorothy: I don't know about you, but
in many ways, aside from the braids and the blue gingham jumper
(not a good look for me), I identified with her. We definitely had
that "fear of surrendering" in common. I feared that surrendering
would be the end of my dreams. She ended up in the odd city of
Oz in her search for a bigger, better life—a life, somewhere over
that rainbow, that she thought for sure would be filled with freedom. For me, that bigger, better life was the secular media world.
I could not imagine what could be better than being at the most
influential news station in my hometown. So I worked weekends,
nights, and holidays. Any time the assignment desk called, I was
off to the races—full speed ahead, without giving a second thought
to the fact that I was spending more time with my colleagues than
with my husband and family. I pushed God and my marriage
aside, running toward my own version of Oz, somewhere over
that idolized idea of the rainbow. And like Dorothy, the further
I wandered, the more I realized that I wasn't in Kansas anymore
and needed to find my way back.

EWTN foundress Mother Angelica tells us to take the steps,
one at a time, closer and closer to Christ. Sometimes that queasy
feeling in the stomach will temporarily stop us in our tracks. But
we are not alone. Dorothy had her friends. The Lion, the Tin Man,

and the Scarecrow, and oh yes, Toto too, helped her to summon the strength to do what she needed to do. In addition to our families and friends, Jesus gives us the saints, the sacraments, and two thousand years of solid teaching to help us out of our own version of the scary witch's castle.

My prayer for you is that you will use all the graces you have been given and realize, as Dorothy did, that if you ever go looking for your heart's desire, there is no need to wander off aimlessly in fear. Remember that "surrender" is most definitely not a four-letter word. Everything we need is in Christ and His Church. I pray that you continue to throw yourself at the foot of the crucifix, into the loving arms of our sweet Jesus. And remember, there really is no place like our home—the one, holy, catholic, and apostolic Church.

Jesus is giving you
such an opportunity
to be holy, holier
than all the saints
who have ever been,
because the world
is in such need
of shining lives,
beacons to see by.

MOTHER ANGELICA

CHAPTER 4

BEAUTY

Fr. Joseph Mary Wolfe, MFVA

A few times in my priestly life of almost three decades I have given dispirited young women my "beauty secrets for ladies." With a smile, I tell them that I have a three-part formula that will, without a doubt, enhance their beauty: *a smile, modesty, and virtue.* It works.

Recently, a religious sister from a family I know well told me the story of how her mother, when she was in her teenage years, was encouraged to enter a beauty contest in the city in which she lived, and winning that contest, she went on to the competition for the state of Louisiana. After being evaluated primarily according to her physical appearance and attributes, she resolved never to put her daughters through such an experience. She encouraged them rather to develop their talents, to study, and to practice virtue so as to attain interior beauty. Her five daughters developed their personalities and their femininity through modesty, living the Catholic Faith, reading, study, musical instruction, and healthy social events. Today, they are vibrant women who are living their vocations to motherhood and religious life fully, faithfully, and fruitfully.

What makes you, O child of God and daughter of the Father, a person worthy of being loved? Physical perfection? The attention of the opposite sex? Likes on social media? Applause on a talent show?

Think deeply about this question, my dear sister, because some of those thoughts may be lingering in the back of your mind and hampering your joy and your genuine love of yourself as God loves you. God thought of you—delighted in the thought of you—and desired not only for you to exist for a few short years on this earth but also to be with Him always, sharing in His life and love forever. And so He *loved* you into existence. That, my dear sister, is what makes you a person worthy of being loved. You are *lovable* because you are made in the image and likeness of God, Who is love.

You know yourself somewhat (but far from totally). Others know a part of you (from their incomplete experience of you). But God knows you completely, without anything unknown or hidden from His loving glance, and He, through St. John the Apostle, assures you of His care: "So we have known and believe the love that God has for us" (1 John 4:16). "We love, because He first loved us" (1 John 4:19). Pope Benedict, commenting on this passage, wrote: "He has loved us first and He continues to do so."

> Nor has the Lord been absent from subsequent Church history: he encounters us ever anew, in the men and women who reflect his presence, in his word, in the sacraments, and especially in the Eucharist. In the Church's Liturgy, in her prayer, in the living community of believers, we experience the love of God, we perceive his presence and we thus learn to recognize that presence in our daily lives. *He has loved us first and he continues to do so*; we too, then, can respond with love. God does not demand of us a feeling which we ourselves are incapable of producing. He loves us, he makes us see and experience his love, and since he has "loved us first," love can also blossom as a response within us.[4]

[4] Pope Benedict XVI, encyclical *Deus Caritas Est* (December 25, 2005), no. 17, emphasis added.

St. Francis of Assisi said that we are what we are before God. Our Father knows us better than we know ourselves, and Jesus, His Son, taught us to call Him *Father*. Mother Angelica and many others have taught that God loves us as though no one else exists. That is hard for us to grasp and to accept, but there are no limits or boundaries to God's love; He is therefore able to know and love us uniquely since we have been uniquely created by Him and are enabled to love and glorify Him uniquely.

Bl. Chiara Badano lay in a hospital bed, sick with painful bone cancer and bald from chemotherapy. And yet people, including clergy, wanted to visit her. They went in order to "visit the sick" but perhaps even more so to come into contact with true beauty, the beauty of a soul radiant with the glory of the One Who is beauty. A cardinal once asked Chiara the secret of her radiant smile. She replied that she offered everything to Jesus: "If You want it, Jesus, so do I." Chiara, in fact, was given the nickname Luce, meaning "light."

Chiara's name in English is Clare. St. Clare of Assisi was canonized just two years after her death. In 2010, Pope Benedict XVI, in his Wednesday catechesis, spoke of St. Clare, quoting words of Pope Alexander IV spoken at St. Clare's canonization:

> In the Convent of San Damiano, Clare practiced heroically the virtues that should distinguish every Christian: humility, a spirit of piety and penitence and charity. Although she was the superior, she wanted to serve the sick sisters herself and joyfully subjected herself to the most menial tasks. In fact, charity overcomes all resistance and whoever loves joyfully performs every sacrifice. Her faith in the Real Presence of Christ in the Eucharist was so great that twice a miracle happened. Simply showing them the Most Blessed

Sacrament distanced the Saracen mercenaries, who were on the point of attacking the convent of San Damiano and pillaging the city of Assisi.

Such episodes, like other miracles whose memory lives on, prompted Pope Alexander IV to canonize her in 1255, only two years after her death, outlining her eulogy in the Bull on the Canonization of St. Clare. In it we read:

How powerful was the illumination of this light and how strong the brightness of this source of light. Truly this light was kept hidden in the cloistered life; and outside them shone with gleaming rays; Clare in fact lay hidden, but her life was revealed to all. Clare was silent, but her fame was shouted out. (*FF*, 3284)

And this is exactly how it was, dear friends: those who change the world for the better are holy, they transform it permanently, instilling in it the energies that only love inspired by the Gospel can elicit. The Saints are humanity's great benefactors![5]

Jesus said, "I am the Light of the world" (John 8:12); He also said, "You are the light of the world" (Matt. 5:14) and "Let your light so shine before men, that they may see your good works and give glory to your Father who is in heaven" (Matt. 5:16). Each of us becomes more beautiful, more radiant, when we are enlightened by the One Who is light. We can't hide it. The moon is most beautiful when it is full, when it completely reflects the light of the sun. So it is with us. We are most beautiful when we most completely reflect the light of the *Son*.

---

[5] Pope Benedict XVI, General Audience, September 15, 2010.

Those who have had near-death experiences often speak of the beauty of what they experienced and of the sense of being profoundly loved. They find our human words unable to convey what they experienced. Realize, dear sister, that a spark of eternity is already alive within you, a fire that was ignited at your Baptism, when the Blessed Trinity began to dwell within you. It is a flame that intensifies as you grow in union with the One Who "cast fire upon the earth" and wishes "it were already kindled!" (Luke 12:49).

Mother Angelica grew up in an unhappy family of divorce and single-mother poverty that made her question whether God existed and, if He did exist, whether He knew her or cared about her: "I was so engrossed in survival that religion did not affect me.... My faith was not at a high level, if it was at any level at all." But then she encountered the Lord and His love for her: "When the Lord came in and healed me through the Little Flower, I had a whole different attitude. I knew there was a God; I knew that God knew me and loved me and was interested in me. I didn't know that before. All I wanted to do after my healing was to give myself to Jesus."[6]

Having worked at EWTN with Mother Angelica for many years, I witnessed that Mother's deep awareness of God's love for her (and for each one of us) made her a very loving and generous person who was at peace with herself. Whenever visitors asked for her signature, she would write: "Jesus loves you! Mother Angelica." Often at the network, as we waited for Mother to arrive for a meeting, we would joke that there is Eastern Time, Central Time, and Mother Angelica Time! She would inevitably be late for meetings because

---

[6] Raymond Arroyo, *Mother Angelica: The Remarkable Story of a Nun, Her Nerve, and a Network of Miracles* (New York: Doubleday, 2005), 31, 33.

she was giving her undivided attention to someone she had met along the way who was in need of a little of her time.

Mother Angelica, however, often talked about the struggles she had with her "Italian temperament." On one of her live shows, she mentioned that she questioned why she was so impatient at times. She went on to say that she then realized that although she was naturally a generous person, she was not generous with *her time*. She wanted everything done yesterday and did not like to postpone her plans because someone interrupted her with a need. Mother worked on that fault and determined that schedules are good but are secondary to the demands of charity "in the present moment." Attentive to the will of God "in the present moment," she could discern peacefully what should be done *now* and carry it out peacefully.

We seldom live in the present moment. You see, we may live in the past, in anger over what was done to us or in guilt over what we've done. Hence, the past can become a cloud that hangs over us for the rest of our lives. Rather than living in the past, we should put *all* of the past—our faults and those of others—into the ocean of God's mercy and leave it there. We should then be grateful for the mercy of God that has freed us from both guilt and resentment.

On the other hand, we can live in fear of the future, worrying about what may happen, rather than placing our trust in the providence of God. If the Lord cares for us today, we can trust that He will not abandon us tomorrow. He is faithful, and our hope in Him will not be disappointed. We *can* and *should* trust in His providence. Bl. Solanus Casey said, "Shake off excessive worry, and exercise a little confidence in God's merciful providence."

Live in the present moment. Yesterday is gone, tomorrow is yet unborn, and the present moment is all that we have. It is God's gift to us. When Ven. Cardinal Francis-Xavier Nguyễn Văn Thuận was put into a communist prison in Vietnam, he was frustrated that his plans for the Church in Vietnam were indefinitely put on hold. But then, noticing that many of the prisoners were simply counting the days of their imprisonment, a useless activity, he had an inspiration to act differently: to take the present moment and fill it with love. And so he smiled at the prison guards, shared with them about places he had traveled in the world, and even taught them languages. He taught them to sing "Veni Creator Spiritus," the traditional Latin hymn to the Holy Spirit. He was delighted to hear his communist guards singing this as they approached his cell in solitary confinement! Love changes things—most importantly, human hearts, including our own. All you have is the present moment, so why not fill it with the love of God and the love of others? Your own heart will be lifted up. "There is no fear in love, but perfect love casts out fear" (1 John 4:18).

Becoming More Beautiful

Servant of God Fr. John Hardon, S.J., wrote a wonderful article titled "Christ the Miracle Worker in the Eucharist," which is easy to find on the Internet and which I encourage you to read. In it, Fr. Hardon points out that when our Lord walked on this earth, He performed miracles by His divinity working *through* His sacred humanity. Jesus promised that He would be with us "always, to the close of the age" (Matt. 28:20). He remains with us especially in the Holy Eucharist, in which He is present in both His divinity and His sacred humanity. This is how His Eucharistic Presence is distinct from His omnipresence, by which God is present everywhere. Only in the Eucharist is Christ's sacred humanity present. And it is His same sacred humanity, Fr. Hardon tells us, through which He worked miracles when He walked on this earth by laying hands on the sick (Luke 4:40), by speaking (John 11:43), by touching (Matt. 8:3), by being touched (Luke 8:44), and so on. Fr. Hardon writes:

> Christ continues performing miracles in our day. I know of no single statement I can share with you that is more practically important than to be convinced that Christ works and wants to perform miracles in our favor today. And that we can add, for the best of reasons, because Jesus Christ is still on earth. And He promised, "Behold, I am with you all days even to the end of the world."

Fr. Hardon goes on to speak of three types of miracles Christ works through His Eucharistic Presence: intellectual, moral, and physical.

"Intellectual miracles" are those by which light and understanding are given to a soul. I like to use the example of André Frossard, the French atheist who walked into a church to look for a friend during adoration of the Most Blessed Sacrament. He did not know what was going on but later wrote in his book *God Exists: I Have Met Him* of what happened in the course of only a few minutes:

> Everything is dominated by the Presence ... of Him of Whom I would never be able to write His name without fear of harming its tenderness, of Him before Whom I have had the good fortune to be a forgiven child who wakes up to discover that everything is a gift.... God existed and was present.... One thing only surprised me: The Eucharist! Not that it seemed incredible, but it amazed me that Divine Charity would have come upon this silent way to communicate Himself, and above all that He would choose

to become bread, which is the staple of the poor, and the food preferred by children.... O Divine Love, eternity will be too short to speak of You.

"Moral miracles" are those by which strength is given to accomplish remarkable things beyond natural human abilities. Think, for example, of all that St. Teresa of Calcutta and Pope St. John Paul II accomplished and all that a Poor Clare of Perpetual Adoration, Mother Angelica, accomplished. All three had a deep devotion to the Blessed Sacrament and spent hours in adoration of the Lord, really, truly, and profoundly present there. They had something more, or rather Someone more, and were thus enabled and strengthened to accomplish remarkable things.

"Physical miracles" are those by which people have received physical healings. Some of the seventy approved miracles of Lourdes (having been first investigated thoroughly by the Lourdes Medical Bureau) took place through the Lord's Eucharistic Presence. Every day during the pilgrimage season in Lourdes, there is a Eucharistic procession in the evening and a candlelight Rosary procession at night. One of the most recently approved miracles of Lourdes (number 68) involved a Salesian religious sister, Luigina Traverso, F.M.A. She was on a stretcher and had not walked for some time. During the Eucharistic procession, she felt a powerful heat penetrate her body and felt the desire to get on her feet. She was later judged cured by her doctors. The consultant, Professor Claudio Rinaldi, wrote on the cover of her clinical folder: "She came back from Lourdes inexplicably cured."

If I had only one piece of advice to give people, it would be this: "Get as close as you can to the Eucharist! If you can receive Holy Communion more often than on Sundays and holy days, do it! If you can spend time in adoration, do it! It will change your life."

I sincerely believe that and will be eternally grateful to the Poor Clares of Perpetual Adoration for teaching me that lesson through their own love for and devotion to the Most Blessed Sacrament.

Do you sometimes need light to guide your path in life? Do you need an intellectual miracle? Go before the tabernacle, and the Lord will give you light.

Do you at times feel overwhelmed by life, burdened and troubled and at the end of your rope? Do you need a moral miracle? Go before our Eucharistic Lord, and He "will give you rest" (Matt. 11:28). He will renew your strength and help you to take the next step forward.

We are all broken earthen vessels in need of healing in a number of ways. Jesus, the Divine Physician, is present in the Eucharist. It is there that we will find healing through the remedy that He sees will most benefit us in this life and especially in the life to come.

Get as close as you can to the Eucharist!

Dear sister, you probably did not expect to find in this chapter a formula for beauty from a priest, but if we understand what true beauty is and its source—namely, He Who is beauty—then it makes sense that a minister of Christ would seek to encourage you in this way. A smile, modesty, and virtue. It works!

I need to be
detached from
my own opinions
in order to be
open to the quiet
inspirations of the
Holy Spirit. Only
then will I be able
to discern what
He is saying and
what He desires.

MOTHER ANGELICA

CHAPTER 5

WHOM SHALL I PLEASE?

Catherine Hadro

My mentor, January, repeated something to me during our Zoom call as hot tears streamed down my cheeks. We were meeting for our weekly virtual check-in, and I was enduring my first overwhelming experience with online critics, or—more bluntly—with online trolls. At that moment, it was essential for me to hear exactly what January was telling me:

"I need you to have the resilience of a saint."

For more than two years, I had hosted a global television show that I founded and launched in early 2017: *EWTN Pro-Life Weekly*. I reported on pro-life issues from a Catholic perspective and also responded to examples of attacks on the sanctity of life—attacks from what St. John Paul II called the "culture of death." Stories that illustrate our culture of death today include those of D.C. police officers claiming they were forced to get abortions or lose their jobs, a child with disabilities in the United Kingdom being deprived of life-saving care because the hospital refused to transfer him, and celebrities wearing Planned Parenthood pins as they sashayed down the red carpet at the Academy Awards.

That is why in June 2019, when singer Miley Cyrus—seemingly naked—publicly shared a photo of herself licking a cake with the phrase "Abortion is healthcare" spelled out in icing for a Planned Parenthood collaboration, I felt compelled to respond. My heart sank on seeing this young woman, filled with astounding talent and inherent dignity, teaming up with the abortion industry and believing the lie that somehow abortion, the killing of an unborn baby, is required for women's health or advancement. Whether Miley intended it or not, the image mocked and distorted a woman's true vocation as a nurturer of life.

I had an idea how I'd respond. I swung by the local grocery store on my way home and picked up a vanilla cake with pink icing. The next day, I posted on all my social media accounts a photo of myself holding a cake with the phrase "Pro-life is pro-woman" written on it and with this caption: "Miley Cyrus, I'd love to have a slice with you and chat about how you can't have a birthday cake when there isn't a birthday. #ProLifeIsProWoman."

Immediately the notifications took off. A majority of the responses on Instagram were positive and from fellow pro-lifers. But the response on Facebook was overwhelmingly vitriolic. The post received more than 3,500 shares—mostly people mocking the pro-life message—but it was the more than 12,000 comments that were truly vile.

Strangers cursed at me, leaving comment after comment that they would dedicate their next abortion to me. One person replied with a photo of a cake that had "Nobody loves you" spelled out in icing. Some people shared messages such as "Abortion sends babies to God faster." It was pure mockery of life, and it was clear to me that those voices were not coming from God. I had apparently swung and hit a hornet's nest, and each comment was an attempt to sting me. I decided not to read through every comment because I knew it would not be healthy for either my spirit or my mind.

The comments from strangers did not affect me to the same degree as messages from close friends, however. Out of respect for those people, I will not share any specifics, but I will say that getting hostile texts from loved ones deriding me for my pro-life post felt like a dagger in the chest. The social media comments bruised my heart, but messages from people I knew ripped it wide open.

It was on that June day that I found myself crying during a Zoom call with my mentor. I felt attacked and misunderstood by so many people who didn't know me, and I felt betrayed by those who did. I thought I would need to be strong for our call, but January could see my pain and told me to cry it out. I'm so grateful for her motherly intuition at that moment and for loving me in that way. I'm also grateful that she did not let me live in that sorrow but helped me to see its higher purpose as she repeated, "I need you to have the resilience of a saint." I then envisioned myself putting on armor like St. Joan of Arc. St. Joan fought a physical war, but I felt as if I were fighting a spiritual one.

I was reminded that day that in the pursuit of holiness, we need to keep our eyes focused on Christ and move forward in our mission, despite what the world and others are saying around us. It sounds trite to say that we need to have thick skin to be a saint—that's not quite it—but we cannot be preoccupied with others' opinions over God's will.

Jesus tells us, "If the world hates you, know that it hated me before it hated you" (John 15:18). And St. Paul says, "Do not be conformed to this world, but be transformed by the renewal of your mind, that you may prove what is the will of God, what is good and acceptable and perfect" (Rom. 12:2). It is a discipline to keep our eyes on Christ and no one else.

This lesson is difficult for me to put into practice. It's one I need to learn over and over again, as I've long classified myself as the classic "people pleaser." Perhaps you can relate to this. I have the hardest time saying no. I neglect my own needs for the sake of others and always strive for perfection. If you asked my Catholic therapist, she would explain that my desire to please others is wrapped up in my childhood wounds. It's all tied to issues of identity and trust. I acted as a people pleaser as a survival mechanism throughout my life, and I'm just now slowly learning to adapt my ways, to draw boundaries, and to be okay with disappointing others. Disappointing others—ouch! It hurts just to type that.

When Crystalina Evert reached out to me about her book and asked if there was a spiritual insight I'd like to offer women, what came to mind is this very spiritual lesson I grapple with. The insight I would like to offer you—especially my fellow perfectionists and people pleasers—is that you must put to death your desire to please others and focus on pleasing God alone. This is not to say that you may intentionally hurt others or quickly brush aside their feelings and opinions, but you cannot place them before God.

Learning to say no to others and yes to God will free you and empower you to be the best version of yourself. I'll share how this is true in my life. When I constantly put others' demands and needs over my own, I end up falling short in my vocation as a wife. The day my husband and I received the sacrament of Matrimony was truly was the most sacred day of my life, as the two of us were transformed into one in that unbreakable covenant: my husband's life became my own. I know that the Lord wants me to prioritize my marriage and to be my husband's support, but I have less energy to serve my husband when I am scheduling every minute of my day for people outside of our home.

"Sorry, honey, can you make dinner for us again? I'll be tied up until late in the evening." Let me be clear: I don't believe it's solely up to wives to cook for their families and execute all the household chores, but I am certainly obligated to be my husband's helpmate and not to leave him stranded with all the responsibilities. My priority needs to be God first, followed by my husband. I love the Lord by loving my husband. Your state in life should provide razor-sharp clarity as to what your priorities should be today.

I imagine this lesson is all the more critical for you readers who are mothers. And as for my single sisters, I see you. I know what it's like to be a young, single Catholic professional who feels as if you don't have an excuse to say no because you don't have the obligations of a spouse or a child. But your health and well-being and boundaries matter. You cannot be a slave to work and to friends' demands. You are called to be the best version of yourself, and that requires drawing boundaries. You are called to make space for God. Do not wait until you're married to draw those boundaries. Take it from me.

Having this mindset has helped me to prune away the opinions and chatter of others. But I have not fully reached detachment from what the world says. It's something I've been striving for, particularly in my time as a television host.

It was in the fall of 2016 that I was offered the position of founding host and producer of *EWTN Pro-Life Weekly*. I was only twenty-six when the show aired in early 2017. It was the greatest honor bestowed on me at the time, and I worked diligently to craft a global television show that would reflect the Church's teachings on life. Prior to my role as host, I had been working as a reporter and producer for *EWTN News Nightly*. I thought I knew exactly what to expect in the transition from reporter on one show to host of another within the network, but I had missed a key difference: I would now be solely focused on pro-life issues.

When I was a reporter for *EWTN News Nightly*, I worked on a variety of topics—not only abortion but also immigration, political campaigns, updates from the Vatican, and more. The people in my life were proud of me; they knew someone who worked as an international news reporter, and it happened to be for the global

Catholic network, the largest religious media network in the world. Even acquaintances who were not Catholic could respect that. But when I announced that I would be hosting a show dedicated to the pro-life cause, I noticed a sudden change in tone from people in my life. I began hearing criticism from some friends and family members. Conversations centering on my job became uncomfortable, and if you live in Washington, D.C., most conversations, unfortunately, center on your job. Having people judge and critique aspects of my work's mission was new to me, and as glamorous as it is to be on TV, my reputation took a hit in some people's eyes. And I knew that from then on, I would always be associated with one of the most divisive issues of our time and that some people wouldn't be able to get past that.

An unseen shift also took place. For as long as I could remember, I had described myself as someone who woke up and heard the birds chirping, but that changed shortly after I took on my new role. Leading up to *EWTN Pro-Life Weekly*'s launch, I pored over books and documents about *Roe v. Wade*, the history of abortion and contraception, and papal encyclicals dealing with life issues. Suddenly, my days were spent thinking, reading, and discussing the gruesome practice of abortion—the intentional killing and dismembering of our smallest and most vulnerable humans. I could feel a heaviness take over, and my husband, Matt, who was my boyfriend at the time, could sense it as well. I learned quickly that I would need a spiritual director if I was going to report and comment solely on pro-life issues. When I first met with my spiritual director at the time and told him about my new job, he agreed that I would need to be focused on prayer. He also commented that I would need to learn how to be detached from people's thoughts and opinions. He was right then, and he is right today.

The criticism I face is not solely from pro-abortion voices. Throughout my five years as host, I have had strangers write me letters and e-mails, calling me immodest—when the only skin showing was my hands and my face. I've had Catholic viewers disagree with pro-life discussion topics on the show. I've slowly learned to expect that I can't please everyone, if anyone.

I am still a work in progress, but I need to share what has been necessary as I attempt to shed my "people-pleaser" and "perfectionist" ways—or I should say, *Who* has been necessary: Jesus of Nazareth. Jesus was not a people pleaser. He was not nailed to the Cross because He was a people pleaser. He did not tell people what they wanted to hear. He was solely concerned with speaking the truth and obeying His Father's commands. He is a sobering reminder of our mission, and He tells us Himself in the Gospel of John, "If you were of the world, the world would love its own; but because you are not of the world, but I chose you out of the world, therefore the world hates you" (15:19). Jesus' wounds are visible proof of the world's hatred for Him. His Resurrection reminds us that the world's wounds are not the end.

The Gospels include example after example of people being offended by Jesus' words and actions because they did not fit the mold they held for Him.

> The Pharisee was astonished to see that he did not first wash before dinner. (Luke 11:38)

> They watched him, to see whether he would heal him on the sabbath, so that they might accuse him. (Mark 3:2)

And in the Gospel of John, when the Pharisees and the scribes approached Jesus with a woman caught in adultery, with the expectation that they could stone her, Jesus responded:

Let him who is without sin among you be the first to throw
a stone at her. (8:7)

Jesus is an expectation breaker. He did not live bound by what
other people had planned for Him. He was and is and always will
be concerned only with His Father's plan.

The slave is never above his master, so we should expect the
same shock from others if we follow the Lord's path. If your pursuit
of God's will ruffles feathers, please know that you are in good
company. Do not be disturbed by others' reactions, but move forward in your discernment. We must follow Jesus' example, and we
must continue to receive Jesus in Communion so that, as John the
Baptist said, "He must increase, but I must decrease" (John 3:30).

In my efforts to avoid disappointing others, I often overextend
and overwork myself. I feel the need to do everything as flawlessly
as possible. In my pride, I have quit sports and hobbies that didn't
come naturally to me. But living for perfection is draining, and
it is not holy. I think back to a piece of wisdom my first spiritual
director shared with me back in college; she would often say, "Mary
burned the toast," speaking of the Blessed Virgin Mary. What my
spiritual director meant is that holiness does not require perfection-
ism. I can be a saint and burn the toast. I can be a saint and not
get straight As. I can be a saint and not throw a Pinterest-perfect
party. Meeting others' expectations of perfection is not necessary
for salvation.

This truth is a thread that runs through the saints' lives. Consider another witness who blocked out people's ideas and comments in her journey to Heaven: St. Catherine of Siena. In a 2018
talk hosted by the Thomistic Institute at Harvard University, Sr.
Mary Madeline Todd, O.P., lectured on the wisdom of this four-
teenth-century lay Dominican. In describing this saint's holiness,

Sr. Mary Madeline told how St. Catherine spent years taking care of a woman who had cancerous tumors. This woman was said to be so horrific that no one wanted to come near her, but St. Catherine personally attended to and nursed her. For whatever reason, this woman—instead of being grateful—was irritated with St. Catherine, and she began to spread atrocious rumors around town that St. Catherine was sexually promiscuous. In the midst of these scandalous rumors, St. Catherine continued to care for the woman when no one else would. Ultimately, the woman had a profound conversion because of St. Catherine's witness. This Doctor of the Church quieted the voices around her—including the voice that originated the atrocious rumors—and followed through in her mission, which ultimately glorified God.

As I shared earlier, when I accepted my job with *EWTN Pro-Life Weekly*, I had to learn to distance myself from people's opinions and to accept disappointing others. I'm learning that lesson all over again now as I've transitioned away from that role and into my new role as an EWTN news contributor. When I accepted the *EWTN Pro-Life Weekly* job, some people asked me, "How could you take that job?" Now, as I leave, others ask me, "How could you leave that job?"

The reason for this change is quite simple: I discerned that God is asking me to trust Him and that it was time to step away. While the discernment was a real wrestle with God, the clarity and peace that came with the decision was overwhelming. I cling to that truth as I am peppered with questions today. Admittedly, I feel at times unsettled with the idea of walking away from hosting a global television show—what had long been my childhood dream. But when those doubts and insecurities creep in, I am reminded of God's reassuring voice. And I know that His voice is the one to which I must listen.

A soul that trusts
God is invincible.

MOTHER ANGELICA

CHAPTER 6

LIVING WITHIN THE FIATS

Sr. Bethany Madonna, SV

My community has a friend in Manhattan, Benedict, who suffers from a genetic disorder that has required countless surgeries throughout his life. The kid is brilliant, and his eyes are always fixed on Jesus. One day, when he was about six years old, Benedict came to our convent to meet the new Sisters. As he met each one, he would comment on their patron saint. But when he came to Sr. Fiat, he looked at his mom, stumped. "Fiat? Who is *Fiat?*"

His mom answered him with a question: "Benedict, tell me, what were God's first words in the book of Genesis?"

"Let there be light."

"Exactly. In Latin, *fiat lux*. And what did Mary say in response to the angel Gabriel?"

"Be it done unto me."

"Yes, *fiat mihi*. And do you remember Jesus' words to His Father before His Passion?"

"Not my will but Yours be done."

"Correct again! *Fiat voluntas tua*. That is what *fiat* means."

Benedict looked back at Sr. Fiat, took her by the hand, and gave her a handshake that went up her entire arm, as if to say, "Congratulations on the best name ever!"

Fiat lux: Let there be light!
From all eternity, God spoke a *fiat* over you, a "Let there be ... you!" A yes was spoken over your life, your existence, your heart,

your love. You were conceived in the heart of God before your parents knew you would come to be.

This reality lights up every aspect of life.

Consider the beauty of the earth, which gives us a window into the Divine Artist, Who fashioned it all with such care. Look at the bright whiteness of the moon with its shadows, the ocean and its crashing waves with innumerable shades of green and blue. See the flowers of the hydrangea—each an exquisite bouquet within itself! Yet all of these things pale in comparison with the human person.

The human person, male and female, is the crown of creation, and it is in the human person that the material and the spiritual meet. Every person is unique and bears a reflection of the divine image. There are so many eye colors, hair types, skin tones, voices, and laughs. And beyond the exterior lies a great mystery, whole vistas, caverns, and uncharted terrain within our minds and hearts. These realms of thought, imagination, intellect, and will are also sacred spaces, distinct and particular to the individual.

And yet as different as we are, every human person shares a longing for happiness, for togetherness, for love. We are made in the image and likeness of the triune God—Father, Son, and Holy Spirit—Who is a communion of Persons, an eternal exchange of love. We come by this longing for communion honestly! We have an insatiable desire for love. We desire to belong, to know, and to be known in a total way. All of our desires for fulfillment are geared toward Heaven.

God knows us in our depths; our heart's most secret recesses are not hidden from Him. Psalm 139 is an expression of the reverence with which we are called to approach every person: "O Lord, you have searched me and known me.... You knit me together in my mother's womb. I praise you, for I am fearfully and wonderfully made" (vv. 1, 13-14, NRSV). God loves the one He creates! It is a marvel to consider. Why you? Why me? How deeply God loves you! He has a plan for each person, and it is as unique to you as your fingerprints are.

Our value is intrinsic, and our worth is not found in what we are able to do, what we own, what we look like, our successes, our accomplishments, or the esteem of others. We have to realize that the culture has told us since we were in kindergarten that we are what we do, achieve, and produce: that we have to meet the expectations, perform the tasks, get the job, make the money, earn the prestige, be beautiful, be stylish, be "in the know"—and that will give us our worth. But what does it do? It leaves us empty, frustrated, dissatisfied, and discouraged.

Here is the reality: no matter what happens to me in this short life, I am a beloved daughter of the heavenly Father, Who sent His only Son to save me. I do not deserve His mercy or His grace, but I receive it as a gratuitous gift. These are holy mysteries!

This is the truth that sets our hearts free to be, free to receive, and free to love.

You are deeply loved.

Fiat mihi: Behold, I am the handmaid of the Lord;
   be it done unto me according to thy word.
I was spending time with middle schoolers, and one of them raised her hand with a more profound question than the typical "Do you wear pajamas?" and "What's your favorite ice cream flavor?" She asked, "Do you have a favorite encounter with God?"

In the life of faith, God enters in, makes Himself present, and even surprises us! He encounters us, gets our attention, and speaks the word that only He knows we need to hear.

God deeply desires you to know and experience His love, and He longs to receive *yours*, because you are the only you; you are the only one who can love Him with this love. And your love changes the course of history.

Every time we pray the Hail Mary, we remind Our Blessed Mother of the moment that changed the trajectory of her life and of salvation history! "Hail Mary, full of grace, the Lord is with thee."

Her response was: "Be it done unto me."

She said yes, not knowing what was to come, not calculating the cost.

She did not foresee the confusion of St. Joseph, the judgment of neighbors, the smelly stable, the slaughter of the Innocents, the flight to Egypt, or the loss of her child for *days*! (Can you imagine her prayer that first night? "Abba ... I lost Your Son.") She became a widow who witnessed the brutal death of her only Son and later became the mother and pillar of strength for every one of her Son's followers. They needed her.

We have a share in Our Lady's heart. We can relate this experience to our own lives, following our yes to the Lord in discipleship and in our definitive vocations. No, I never foresaw this sorrow, this challenge, this weakness in myself or in my husband or in my children. And for those of us in religious life, we don't know in advance what struggles will arise in our hearts, in our communities, or in the lives of those entrusted to our care.

But we say yes all the same, as Mary did. We begin to walk on the path as it unfolds before us. We say, "I willingly share life with you," with the full understanding that life is a journey, an adventure, an epic poem, a love story, filled with joys and ecstasies, tragedy and sorrow, success and failure, change and growth! Love is always sacrificial and life-giving if it is *real*, if it is truly authentic. It requires a death to our false selves as we rise to a newness of life.

Do you remember in *The Sound of Music* when Maria runs away from the captain because she is in love with him and the

Reverend Mother tells her that loving this man doesn't mean that she loves God any less? The Reverend Mother tells her in song to "climb every mountain." I always find that one line in that song sticks out. The Reverend Mother tells Maria to find her dream, "a dream that will need all the love you can give every day of your life, for as long as you live."

We have to pray for eyes to see disappointments, weakness, regrets, and events that leave us powerless as opportunities to grow in intimacy, to come to maturity, to the full stature of Christ, by way of our faith in God, trusting in what He has promised.

A woman I'll call Catherine shared with me her experience of abortion and how Jesus reached her. Catherine fell away from her Catholic Faith in college, dabbling in other religions and philosophies. She was searching for meaning and love. She fell for a man, and after suffering two abortions with him, broke off the relationship, realizing it was not love.

An aching loneliness and need for God steadily increased in her heart. One day, she was trying out meditation in an ashram, a place of Eastern, yoga-like practices. To her surprise, as she sat in silence, Jesus Christ came to her, right into her meditation. He was wearing a robe that was all white, and he leaned down toward her and extended His hand, saying gently, "Consider me again."

"Consider me again." Catherine journeyed back to the Catholic Church and remembers her first confession after *thirty years*, sobbing. The power of mercy was healing her heart.

Jesus found her and revealed that His love for her is particular and infinite; that His mercy is total, tender, and without limits; and that He had chosen her and wanted her to *choose Him back*.

When we receive God's mercy, when we open our hearts to receive His love in areas of weakness or shame, we are set free and *filled* with His grace, with the joy of the Holy Spirit, and with a deep desire to respond in kind.

The enemy wants us to keep things in the dark, in bondage. But the antidote to shame is to bring things into the light and humbly to seek help. So, if alcohol is an issue for you or a family member, reach out to AA or Al-Anon for encouragement and support. If pornography or masturbation is present in your life, bring this to the light and seek accountability. Jesus wants us to be free. Go to Confession regularly, receive Holy Communion as often as you can, use Covenant Eyes or blocks on your computer, restrict your TV and computer use to public rooms of your house, or revert to a flip phone! Fast from a food or drink you really like. Learning to say no to yourself in little ways will help you to gain self-mastery, which will increase your confidence and self-respect. Never give in to discouragement, because God's mercies are always new and nothing is beyond Him.

Fiat voluntas tua: Thy will be done.

As women, we can be hard on ourselves. By not accepting that we are poor sinners in need of mercy and grace, we rebel against reality. We need a Savior. We do further injustice to others by holding them to unrealistic and impossible standards. We will always fall short, and others will always disappoint us. What's the answer then? "Love is patient and kind.... Love bears all things, believes all things, hopes all things, endures all things" (1 Cor. 13:4, 7).

Love "hopes all things." What does it mean to live in joyful hope?

St. Paul said this: "Forgetting what lies behind and straining forward to what lies ahead, I press on toward the goal for the prize of the upward call of God in Christ Jesus" (Phil. 3:13–14). He could have lamented, "Woe is me!" but he didn't. We, for our part, have to accept the forgiveness and mercy we have been offered so lavishly! When our Lord appeared to St. Faustina and asked her to tell the world about His ocean of mercy, He told her to encourage everyone to place all their trust in His mercy, saying, "Jesus, I trust in You."

He sees us; He knows us. Do we realize this?

You may remember the scene in the Gospel when Jesus goes to dine at the home of Simon the Pharisee (Luke 7:36-50). A sinful woman comes in and washes Jesus' feet with her tears, dries them with her hair, and anoints them with costly ointment. Simon is disgusted and thinks, "If only He knew what kind of woman this was who is touching Him!"

Knowing Simon's thoughts, Jesus says to him, "Do you see this woman?"

Jesus sees her.

Every act of hers is so distinctly feminine: the tears, the hair, the kisses, the ointment. Jesus receives her. He receives her tears of repentance and gratitude. The hair that crowns her head is set at His feet in adoration, making a gift of her loveliness. The precious ointment is used to seal her kisses of love.

And Jesus sees *you*.

He sees your tears, your laughter, your goodness, your thoughtfulness—the ways you reach out to others and respond to their needs. He sees the many tender expressions of affection and movements of selfless love you show Him. Jesus sees you and looks on you with love.

Nothing is wasted on Jesus. Matthew's Gospel tells of a woman who poured ointment on Jesus' head, and the others who were present asked, "Why this waste?" (26:8). And you may hear the same: "What a waste! Staying at home with your children when you're so talented!" or "Not going out to bars or clubs when you're so fun!" or the ridiculous thought of "throwing your life away as a religious Sister!"

Now, what did Jesus say as a rebuke to those who criticized the woman who anointed Him? "She has done a beautiful thing to me" (Matt. 26:10)—one that will not be forgotten until the end of time.

Jesus never forgets our acts of love. He treasures us without measure, regardless of our sins or failings. When we go to Confession with sincere and repentant hearts, we are not spurned. Jesus receives us like the father of the prodigal son, running to meet us and smothering us with kisses.

We can begin to live in hope by letting Jesus into the dark corners of our hearts, the places we like to pretend He doesn't know about. I'm convinced that in every family, there is one closet that everyone knows is there, but just the thought of opening the door leaves everyone exhausted and depressed. We can think, "It is going to take so much time and energy to sort through that stuff! It's going to be a bigger mess before it gets organized. I'd rather not even look at it." This is precisely where Jesus wants to go—these rooms in the heart—for our own freedom. "For freedom Christ has set us free" (Gal. 5:1).

Before His Passion, Jesus said, "For this reason the Father loves me, because I lay down my life. . . . No one takes it from me, but I lay it down of my own accord" (John 10:17-18). Jesus loves us freely and gave Himself up for us. In His self-gift, He desires to heal us, free us, and fill us with the strength of His joy. We can imitate Jesus in trusting the Father and submitting our will, our preference, and our perceptions. "In His will is our peace."[7] As we pray in the Litany of Trust, "Your plan is better than anything else."

---

[7] "E'n la sua volontade è nostra pace." Dante Alighieri, *Paradiso* 3, 85.

A few years ago, Patty came into the lives of us Sisters. When her boyfriend found out she was pregnant, he gave her an ultimatum: "You pick: me or the baby." Crushed and betrayed, she chose her child and moved into the convent with us. Although raised a Buddhist, she would come into our chapel for Holy Hour. She would look at Jesus, and during this time, He began to heal her heart, silently speaking the truth about her dignity, His plan for love, and her beauty. Her son was born two months premature, and fearful for his health, Patty asked that he be baptized a Catholic at the hospital and given the name Patrick Joseph. He was put into neonatal intensive care, and he rocked it! Patty realized that if this is what she wanted for him in death, this is what she wanted for them both in life. She began going to RCIA classes to enter the Church. One of the other guests living with us was so taken by Patty's joy, she said, "I'm going with Patty to class tonight."

When Patty's student visa was up, she decided to return to Thailand. She mentioned that to the priest preparing her for the sacraments, and he said she was ready for Baptism and First Holy Communion. The night before she was to receive the sacraments, she and I shopped for her baptismal garment. Let me paint the picture for you: Manhattan. Macy's. Thanksgiving weekend. 9:00 p.m. Closing time in an hour. We ran in, and Sr. Rita and Patty went one way, and I ran the other with Patty's three-month-old baby in my arms. There I was, rifling through the dress rack. I'm not sure what I looked like—a Sister in full habit, dress shopping with an infant, at night—but a guy who worked there approached cautiously and asked, "Can I help you, Sister?"

"Yes. You can pray we find the perfect white dress for that young woman's Baptism!"

And did he ever! It was gorgeous! It fit her as if it were made just for her. The young man picked shoes to match and rang up the purchase at a generous discount. It was like a dream. When we got home, Patty asked if we had a little chapel veil for her to wear.

Patty said, "Sister, my heart is pounding so fast. I feel like tomorrow is my wedding day."

And it was. God wed Himself to her soul in Baptism. Then Jesus gave Himself to her in Holy Communion. "This is my Body … given up for you."

Jesus gives Himself totally for us, and in this He gives us the strength to withstand any trial. We are never, ever alone on the crosses in our lives, no matter what.

During His Passion, the crowd shouted to Jesus, "Come down now from the cross!" (Matt. 27:42). When we find ourselves united to Christ, living out the sacrificial love that will make us whole and free, we can hear this temptation as well: "This is too hard. What's the point? You're too tired; you'll fail. Just come down from the cross."

In dying, Jesus destroyed our death, and in rising, He fully restored our life. So, too, in dying to our self-love and selfish inclinations, we not only rise to a new life with Him, but we soar.

What does this look like practically, to be united to Jesus? It is to experience Christ dwelling within you, making every aspect of your life intercessory. We can offer anything and everything, highs and lows, to the Lord as prayer. This can become our habit of thought: Jesus, I offer this to You. I offer You this project at work, this late night, this illness, this load of laundry, this temptation, this apology, this diaper, this date, this loneliness, this Rosary. And for whom? For your four-year-old son's future wife; for a woman at the bedside of a dying parent; for my husband's healing; for the isolated and lonely; for that couple's perseverance; for freedom from this addiction; for the teenager tempted to have an abortion. The list goes on and on and on.

Conclusion

To close, I want to share with you the story of a young woman who came on retreat with us:

> I didn't have the relationship a girl needs to have with her father. I had several broken relationships and had seen a lot of abuse. I didn't know who I was. I felt unlovable, and yet I still wanted to give myself away. I decided to go on a young women's retreat at Villa Maria Guadalupe. It was called "Perfect Love Casts Out Fear," and I really wanted to believe that was true. My relationship with God at the time was not a personal one.
>
> One of the Sisters gave a conference on "The Feminine Genius" and the dignity of being a woman made in the image and likeness of God. She described woman as the crowning glory of creation, and something happened to me. I realized that woman was the last touch, the cherry on the cake, if you will. It dawned on me: "I have so much to give!" God made everything, all these things ... and He decided to make me. The world needed *me.*
>
> I went to the Lord in prayer, saying, "Jesus, these are the things I believe about myself. Show me how to be a woman. I need to know the truth about who I am."
>
> I had been living in a world of so much anger, feeling I could never be pure again because of what had happened to me, because I had fallen into sin. That weekend, I knew God was saying, "You have dignity. You do not need to degrade yourself."
>
> I understood then that I needed help, and it wasn't long before I was able to receive God's forgiveness. It made me cry because I knew I wasn't alone anymore. And all

my dreams came back. I had yearned for a fairy tale, for someone to come and save me! I reclaimed my freedom by accepting God's infinite love. I started sitting before the Blessed Sacrament; it was the one place where I felt myself. I would just sit there and allow myself to be loved.

I started living, really living. I wanted to be the woman Christ made me to be. I could love myself and give myself to Him. It was transforming. I now know that I am the daughter of a King. I know that I am beautiful; my body is beautiful. It took sacrifice to live this way. Things changed for me; the way I saw and spoke with others changed. I started to really love people, seeing the good in them. I knew happiness was out there, but the joy of knowing Christ is like a never-ending, eternal fire! What's more, I started wanting to see God, face-to-face; I desired Heaven. Mass is what now gets me through the day, through my life, because at Mass, Heaven comes down to Earth. I can't be thankful enough.

The world needs you to be the woman Christ made you to be. The world needs saints, prophets, and martyrs. The blood of martyrs is the seed of faith. There will be red martyrs. But there will also be white martyrs, martyrs of love, those who respond to the call to lay down our lives like Jesus in all the reality of our lives. What does this look like?

It looks like kindness in the face of judgmental and cynical comments from people who learn that you're expecting your fifth child.

It looks like not getting invited to the family reunion because you didn't attend that ceremony.

It looks like being forced to quit your job after fourteen years because you could not in good conscience call students by pronouns that do not correspond to their God-given sex.

It looks like breaking up with your boyfriend because you will *not* break your promise to God to save sexual intimacy for marriage.

It looks like hearing, "What a waste!" when discerning a religious vocation.

It looks like placing yourself at the service of the Church in ministry even though it is not popular and the pay is not great.

You can name some yourself: you are living it. That's what it looks like. "Blessed are those who are persecuted" (Matt. 5:10).

Some things are worth dying for. Life and truth are worth dying for. And no one takes my life from me—I lay it down freely! (see John 10:18).

The enemy hates women—creative life bearers, nurturers, other Marys. St. Teresa Benedicta of the Cross (Edith Stein), who spent her last day at Auschwitz comforting mothers, feeding children, and combing their hair, said this: "God combats evil through the power of a woman's maternal love."

We need to live our motherhood—fully, freely, and fiercely.

Think of St. Mother Marianne Cope of Hawaii. She didn't have a cure for leprosy. She had her hands and her feet and a heart overflowing with maternal love. She also happened to have gifts of administration and discernment, a knack for cleanliness and order, an eye for fashion, and an ability to sew beautiful clothes for the girls in her care. She planted fragrant flowers and taught the girls to sing, drawing them out of a life of dissipation and despair into one of sunshine and preparation for death, the door to eternity.

For a more recent example, think of Servant of God Gwen Coniker and her husband, Jerry, of Ohio—parents of thirteen—who founded the Apostolate for Family Consecration to help Catholic families to grow in holiness. You may have heard of Catholic Family Land? We live in a time where husbands and wives, fathers and mothers need support in raising their children to be Spirit-filled disciples in love with Jesus. The Lord revealed to Gwen families' thirst for such support and encouragement, and He placed that on her heart.

Your love matters. You are necessary. The love of your heart changes the world, whether that fact is recognized or not. Hidden love changes the world. Your fiat changes the world. How else do you explain the fact that Thérèse of Lisieux never stepped foot outside her cloistered convent and yet is currently known in every Catholic church around the world—in Vietnam and Ghana and Argentina and America? How did that happen? Love took over, and St. Thérèse didn't dictate to God how it needed to look.

Let Love take over your life, and give God permission to make you a saint—and a great one.

Fiat lux. Fiat mihi. Fiat voluntas tua. Amen.

I want you to have
a new concept of
holiness. You've got
to be holy where
you are: washing
dishes, at the office,
at school. Wherever
you are, you can
be holy there.

MOTHER ANGELICA

CHAPTER 7

CHANGES

Joy Pinto

There aren't too many things that remain constant in life. Actually, the only constant things are God and change. You and I are continually changing, and when we are not changing, then certainly the circumstances around us are.

I was once just a daughter growing up in New Jersey with four sisters and three brothers. My parents, for whom I am grateful, were the only mom and dad I ever had. At the age of nineteen, I married my beloved husband, Jim. Nine months later, I was pregnant with our firstborn son. Nine months after he was born, I was pregnant with a set of twin daughters. Then six years later, I was pregnant with our fourth child—a boy. I started off in New Jersey and moved to Pittsburgh and then to Birmingham, Alabama, where we have lived for forty-one years. How does a girl from New Jersey end up spending more than forty-one years of her life in Birmingham, Alabama? Change!

I know that every circumstance that happens to us on this journey will make us either bitter or better. We always have a choice. We either adjust to the change that is before us and let the change make us into something new, or we resist the change and make life harder for ourselves and all the other people around us. As I sit here and write this, I am sixty-four years old, and I said yes to Jesus at the age of eighteen. I was baptized as an infant in the Lutheran church but never had formal faith formation until a radical conversion in 1976. I have been clay in the Potter's hand for a long time. Sometimes, I have been soft and pliable and, other times, as hard as a rock.

My faith formation started in the Charismatic movement back in the late seventies. I thought I always wanted what God wanted for my life until I knew the cost and the change that it would require of me. Have you ever known what God was asking of you? Are you trying to discern His plan for your life? Even when I didn't know what God was asking of me, I found that it cost me something. Usually it was something that I loved—even a good thing I loved. On our journey to holiness, we should keep in mind what Hebrews 12:1 says to you and me: "Therefore, since we are surrounded by so great a cloud of witnesses, let us also lay aside every weight, and sin which clings so closely, and let us run with perseverance the race that is set before us." It might be drugs, alcohol, sexual promiscuity, or an unhealthy relationship that we must lay aside. Addiction makes you give up everything for one thing: the addiction; recovery is giving up that one thing for everything. God asks you and me: Do you love me more than this one thing?

My first sacrifice was moving away from a family that I loved and thought I needed to live near to survive. I was married all of four weeks and had to tell my parents that we were moving to Pittsburgh to follow God's plan for our lives. I learned that God was taking me up on my marital vows that a man should leave his mother and a woman must leave her home and the two cleave together and become one. Ouch! I wept every night for the first three months, and Jim would hold my face in his hands to comfort my breaking heart as I cried myself to sleep. Change.

God was busy about His plan in my life, creating a need for Him alone. He wants to be everything to us—our strength, our peace, our comfort, our joy, our hope, our love. I thought I needed my family, my parents, my familiar places, but He wanted me to need Him alone, and boy, did I need Him! I read my Bible every day for guidance and direction, and I developed a prayer life that was my lifeline to Him. My life was changing right before my eyes. I knew He loved me, but there were and still are areas in my life that need to come under His authority and His way.

I loved being a wife and mother. I believed I was living out God's plan for my life. We moved to Birmingham when our oldest was sixteen months old and I was seven months pregnant with our twin daughters. When the twins arrived, I had three babies under two and no family in sight. It was just Jim and I, and that is just the way God wanted it. He was making us dependent on Him and on each other. We had a beautiful church family, and they were loving and very kind to us. God was giving us His family, but it was a change that wasn't always easy for me.

Sometimes in life, changes come to us that we are not in control of: death, illness, miscarriages, parents' divorces, failed marriages, unfaithful spouses, loss of a job. Proverbs 13:12 tells us that "hope deferred makes the heart sick, but a desire fulfilled is a tree of life." Some people suffer many things. I am always amazed at the resilience of those who are able to overcome some of life's greatest losses. We as a people of God should believe that God will bring good out of every evil and somehow will write straight with all our crooked lines.

The beauty of being Catholic—and I am a convert—is that our Lord has given us all the sacraments to help us on our faith journey and everything we need to become as holy as we want to be. Mother Angelica would encourage us, "We all are called to be great saints. Don't miss the opportunity." The sacrament of Confession purges us of our souls' wretchedness and reconciles us with God so that we may become better versions of ourselves. Sometimes we tend to make it all more complicated than it really is. We don't like to die to ourselves or to change our attitudes, but pride always has an awful way of manifesting itself when we least expect it.

I know for a fact that my marriage is making me holy. All our relationships are opportunities to change, if we allow God to come in with His light and mercy and help us to see our blindness in any given situation. Jim and I are still on this journey, and you would think that forty-four years in, we would have mastered marriage. Even in marriage, we are changing. Our bodies are different, our health has changed, and our family has changed. I know my body is wasting away, but my spirit is young. My attitudes and beliefs have deepened. I have learned what really is important in life.

As a cancer survivor, I have been to hell and back, and my faith and my person were tested in the process. I would not have missed that journey for anything. It taught me that life is a gift, as is each day, so make the best of it. Don't sweat the small things in life; don't major in the minor things that life throws your way. It is hard to remember that in the frenzy of the moment—say, amid heated words and hurt feelings. But at such times, it is best to pause, step back, and reflect on what has been said. Breathe, practice the virtue of prudence, and think before you speak or respond.

The *Catechism of the Catholic Church*, paragraph 1810, tells us: "Human virtues acquired by education, by deliberate acts and by a perseverance ever-renewed in repeated efforts are purified and elevated by divine grace. With God's help, they forge character and give facility in the practice of the good. The virtuous man is happy to practice them." We never have to do this alone. Our heavenly Father will empower us, assist us, and grant us divine grace to become better versions of ourselves, but we must ask Him: *God help me!* When you receive the Eucharist—the Body and Blood, Soul and Divinity of our Lord—take that time to cry out to Him, asking that you become what you are consuming—more of Jesus and less of you. Give Him your weaknesses, your failings, your pride, your cold and stony heart. Ask Him to give you a heart of clay, pure and holy. He can mold you and make you whole. Change!

My husband, Jim, was an Episcopalian priest for twenty-two years, and looking for truth and authority, he started his reversion to the Catholic Church. I was not on his journey, and for me, it was a crisis of faith. I was happy with my life. Jim started asking me who I thought was in charge of the Church, and whether I thought that God would have left us here to figure everything out on our own, and other such questions. I loved being a pastor's wife, and I loved my church family. God had already asked me to leave father, mother, sister, and brother to follow Him—and I did so, for love of Him. He had given me a new family, and now He was asking me to walk away from them too! I had done that already, and I was not about to do it again.

The journey from Protestant land into Catholic land was painful, to say the least. Change! I remember lying on my bed in a fetal position, crying, and it felt like the pain was coming out of every pore in my body. Cost what it may, did I love Jesus more than this life? It was He who gave me this new family, this new land, this new way of living and being. But He was asking me to walk away from it all and follow Him into a land unknown. How could one comprehend the beauty, truth, and goodness of the Catholic faith in an RCIA program? I felt as if I were in kindergarten. Although I read my Bible every day, there was still so much more to learn and understand. Change!

We entered the Church in 2004, during the pontificate of Pope St. John Paul II, and in 2005, he passed away, our local bishop resigned, and our parish had no priest in residence. One year in, and my Church had no pope, no bishop, and no priest, and yet nothing changed. Mass was celebrated every Sunday by a rotating priest, and although the offices were in transition, the ship stayed afloat. I knew I was Catholic, and the Church stood the test of time yet again.

I was introduced to so many holy men and women of God who had run their race and were now cheering me on. So many of the saints lived such beautiful lives of surrender, sacrifice, and total obedience to our Lord. I have loved learning about their ordinary lives becoming extraordinary and their heroic actions done with such grace and love for our Lord. The saints show us that it is possible, one act at a time, to die to oneself and to choose others over oneself. We can ask the saints to pray for us when we are weak and battling our own demons.

Some of my most difficult times on this faith journey have been raising teenagers and losing the sense of control I thought I had in my children's lives. I learned the hard way that my children, although gifts from God, were only passing through my life. I had them for a time. But they belong to God—not to me. In little ways, God prepares us for detachment. First, it's dropping off your child for three hours for a "mother's day out." Then comes the first day of kindergarten, and you cannot believe your child will make it without you. I remember dropping off our oldest at college; as we drove away, I thought my heart was going to break through my chest wall.

The roles and relationships in which we find ourselves change and require us to change. If you are a parent, unless your children are called to the priesthood or the religious life, they will likely marry, and you might become a mother-in-law and have grandchildren.

I didn't know how to be a mother-in-law. I could no longer just give my advice when it wasn't asked for or give my opinion just because I thought I was right. This was totally new for me. I needed help. I asked a wise Italian woman in my life, and she said, "I am going to tell you what my mother-in-law told me: Minda your owna business." I didn't know how to do that apart from God. I needed help from above. Jesus wants to make us new. He wants to be the foundation of our souls, making us beautiful from the inside out. Our interior life is what matters: how we act, how we speak, how we listen, how we love.

God wants to change our lives. He is asking us to come out into the deep, to trust Him, never to stop saying yes to Him. He wants to make us new. He wants to create in us clean hearts and renew a right spirit within us (see Ps. 51:10). We won't get another chance to live this life. Let us pray that we won't shrink from anything that God asks us to do.

I look back over the years and know that He alone will give us the grace to say yes. My faith on this journey has been tried and tested. 1 Peter 4:12–13 says, "Beloved, do not be surprised at the fiery ordeal which comes upon you to prove you, as though something strange were happening to you. But rejoice in so far as you share Christ's sufferings, that you may also rejoice and be glad when his glory is revealed." I am still running my race. Will there be more trials and sufferings in this life? I suppose so. But it is my hope to suffer well for His glory and always to make change my friend.

The whole essence
of becoming holy
is to do God's will.

MOTHER ANGELICA

CHAPTER 8

BREAKING FREE

Crystalina Evert

For many of us, the sense of inadequacy begins in childhood. I don't know if you're a sexual-abuse survivor like me. Perhaps your story involves physical abuse, divorce, and infidelity, as mine does. Maybe you've suffered through abortion or have wrestled with depression or deep-rooted, hidden addictions. I don't know your story, but what I do know is that you are not alone.

In my case, I learned from my earliest years that:

I was never good enough for my father to stay.

I was never valuable enough to be protected from sexual abuse.

I was never skinny enough for my boyfriends to be faithful.

I was never precious enough not to be hit.

I was never pure enough not to be labeled with degrading names.

If these lies are left unchecked, their effects can last a lifetime.

Years after the toxic relationships in my life ended, I married Jason, and we began raising a family. But it wasn't long before the wounds of my past resurfaced. I felt that I wasn't whole enough to be the wife or mother I needed to be. I felt like a paralytic who was expected to swim. While drowning in an ocean of my inadequacies, I discovered that the betrayal came from within me. The problem wasn't the demands of marriage or motherhood. The problem was that I had never untied the knots that bound me.

Perhaps you have been wounded by someone. Perhaps your wounds have been self-inflicted through your own choices.

Regardless of what happened or when, the past does not dictate your future or your identity. Sometimes, instead of identifying our wounds, we identify ourselves by them. We live out of our wounds. Sometimes we act as if we're empowering ourselves through victimhood. In other words, we refuse to heal so that we need never be accountable for the direction our lives take. Of course, we can always blame our bad choices on something or someone. But this isn't empowerment. It's giving in.

Ladies, it's time to banish whatever tempts us to despair and stands in the way of the life we've always wanted. At some point, we need to slay our insecurities so that they no longer control us. Not only do we need to ditch the fronts we put on for others, hoping they'll think we have it all together, but we also need to drop the masks we constantly show ourselves.

Because the healing process sometimes feels overwhelming or impossible, women are tempted never to begin. I have learned that if you own your wounds, they will have less power over you. If you name the lies, you can take authority over them. But to do this, you need to show up to your fight. Stop saying "I'm fine." What lie do we tell ourselves more than this one? Odds are you've never felt the need to look up the definition of "fine" in a dictionary. But here's what it says: "well or healthy; not sick or injured." When was the last time we felt this way? It was probably quite some time ago, we will likely admit if we're honest with ourselves. However, acknowledging this is more difficult than hiding behind words such as "fine."

We've all done it in our way. Because we don't want to deal with a specific situation—or the memories of it—we escape. We run to something as simple as food or shopping or as serious as drugs, alcohol, or loveless (superficial) relationships. In time, our temporary solutions become permanent crutches that we rely on to cope with life. We cling to them because we want the pain of worthlessness and the feelings of inadequacy that haunt us to stop, even for a moment. In time, those false consolations become an addictive, numbing medicine.

Because I didn't know how to handle the weight and baggage from my past, these coping mechanisms became a vicious cycle for me. I hated being alone and going to bed at night because it seemed like the silence constantly screamed the truth. I felt lost, and the only solution I knew was to distract myself.

Meanwhile, my exterior disposition would fool just about anyone. My life felt like a show for others, and my smiles were nothing but a disguise. Yet this mask only deepened my sense of feeling unknown. I wanted to be loved for what was underneath the mask, but I was afraid to drop it. I eventually realized why I was desperate to cling to the lie that I was "fine." I believed it was unacceptable not to be okay. I had to keep it together. I couldn't fall apart. After all, what will others think?

But here's the truth: you're not fine; neither am I, and that's okay. So, let's get over this unrealistic expectation that our lives should look like a filtered social media pic. Instead of trying to mold our public image to fit a standard of bogus perfection, let's admit our brokenness and move forward to build the life that God intended for us.

I also used to tell myself, "It doesn't matter." Some lies might be hard to see, but this one is not. Exactly what doesn't matter? Do you not matter? Do your dignity and self-worth not matter? Does what happened to you not matter? Although this might be difficult, go back in your memories to when your wounds were caused. As soon as it happened, was your first reaction "Oh, that wasn't a big deal"? Odds are you felt quite the opposite. But because you didn't know what to do with the fact that it mattered so much, you began telling yourself and others that it didn't matter.

I often talked myself out of the reality of what happened to convince myself of a tamer version of the truth. But the first step in healing wounds is to name them and recognize that they matter. Permit yourself to feel your feelings instead of stifling them and thinking that your strength is measured by your capacity to be numb.

What happened to us matters, and we know it. Yet because that reality scares us, we minimize, deflect, and deny. But that won't help. We matter, and because of this, what happened to us matters. To heal, we need to admit this and declare it!

After admitting that I wasn't okay and that my wounds mattered, I reached the point at which I knew something needed to be done. But because my hurts were so deeply personal, I assumed that the best way to solve them would be to handle everything myself.

The first step I took to "deal with it" was to isolate myself and shut out the world. But this only made me weaker. I felt as if I were locked in a room with the devil, imprisoned in solitary confinement with nothing but negative thoughts and feelings of shame. My secrets took control of me, and I became a hostage to myself.

I felt so much pent-up rage from the abuse I had suffered from my father and my boyfriends that I knew it needed an outlet. So I started to channel my anger through kickboxing. But however hard I punched and kicked, I still wasn't dealing with my anger.

No matter what you've been through, you can deal with it, but here's the question: Are you? Or are you refusing to deal with it by hiding it? You need to reject isolation and every false consolation in order to deal with it. After all, you deserve true consolation.

Women often have strong reasons to keep secrets. If you've been betrayed, abused, raped, or molested or have had an abortion, you may think, "No one can know. If I tell anyone, it will be a mess. They'll never look at me the same. It's not worth it." You may fear retaliation or looks of reproach. You might want to cling to your disguise to maintain control of how others view you. If someone in your family abused you, you might fear the chaos that will ensue if the truth is exposed.

But despite all these worries, not only *can* you tell someone what happened—you *must*. Your heart was not created to bear such a burden alone, and your healing is far more important than anyone else's reputation. When people you love are suffering, do you consider them a burden? In the same way, those who love you want to help you feel alive again. But they can't do this if you conceal your wounds. So let go of your fears and remember that feeling whole again is more important than clinging to a good image.

If we keep our wounds locked away, our past will continue to haunt us. We'll feel a constant battle between who we've become and who we want to be. Still, this battle is pivotal in your healing process, and no one can fight it on your behalf. Don't be intimidated. You're stronger than you think. If you need a little extra motivation, consider this: I used to believe that I was protecting myself by remaining silent about my abuse. But my silence only kept me a prisoner to the anger and the unforgiveness.

Don't hesitate to ask God for help at difficult moments. Pray for strength. God accepts you as you are. It doesn't matter how bad your situation is; God is bigger than all of it. Only through Him can you find wholeness and deliverance.

No one wants to admit she's broken and needs a therapist. The idea used to make me think, "How embarrassing!" There is no shame in wanting to be healed, but coming to this realization can be a long journey.

I changed my life and even became a missionary. I met my husband, we married and started our family, and I assumed that all my baggage could be left outside the Church as I entered this new phase of my life. God had given me everything I wanted, and yet one day, I found myself sobbing in the kitchen. I wasn't the wife or the mother I wanted to be. I was often angry and felt inadequate and incapable of giving and receiving love. One of the purposes of marriage is the sanctification of spouses, and this means our faults and wounds will come to the surface to be healed. Mine began seeping to the surface, and they were erupting. I prayed, went to adoration consistently, and knew I had come to a breaking point in my life. I knew in my heart that Jesus was asking me to go to counseling. It was humbling to admit I needed a counselor. I did not want to go, but I knew I had to in order to heal.

One day, Jason walked into the kitchen when I was crying, and he knew what I was feeling. He wrapped his arms around me and said, "Don't worry, honey. You're just under construction." I had to laugh because he was right. I knew it was time to find a good counselor and begin dealing with everything I had swept under the rug for more than a decade. I once heard it said, "You're as sick as your secrets, and your secrets keep you sick." How do you know when it's time to get these secrets out? Here's a list of things to consider. The more of these items you recognize in yourself, the sooner you should find a good counselor:

- Difficulty sleeping
- Recurring nightmares
- Excessive fears
- Traumatic experiences in your past
- An inability to manage emotions in a healthy way
- A perceived need to hide the truth from others
- Significant fluctuations in your mood
- Depression or suicidal thoughts
- Destructive behavior
- A habit of negative self-talk
- Excessive anxiety

ꙮ Fear of aloneness

ꙮ Social isolation

ꙮ Fear of being alone with another

ꙮ Substance abuse or addictions

ꙮ Disruption in your performance at work or school

ꙮ A pattern of instability in your relationships with others

If you can relate to some of these things, take action. To find a good counselor, see the list of websites at womenmadenew.com. You may need to shop around. If one counselor doesn't quite fit, try another. Don't feel obligated to commit to one who doesn't seem right for you. Instead, invest serious effort in this search, and it will pay off. Although this step may seem frightening, it often brings the quickest relief.

The things that happened to me were shameful, but I do not live in shame any longer, and neither should you. Know that you can conquer it! There is no shame in revealing what happened to you so that you can heal and become the woman God created you to be.

It has been said that suffering can make us bitter or make us better. The choice is ours. To become better, we have to accept that healing is a process. Like a physical wound, emotional healing takes time. Scar tissue may remain. But if we don't clean the wound, it can become infected, and the damage can spread. Whether physical or emotional, purifying wounds tends to be an uncomfortable process, but it's essential.

We can cleanse minor wounds ourselves, but the serious ones require help. For these, remember that it's not your job to be the healer. The more serious a physical wound is, the more a patient needs to accept help from another to cure it. Anyone can put on a Band-Aid, but it takes a doctor to operate. Don't reach for a Band-Aid when you need surgery. Instead, have the humility to receive help.

With any serious operation, the patient is likely to feel worse before she feels better. Don't be alarmed if you experience this, and don't assume that you're moving in the wrong direction. You're not. There's a purpose to your pain, and there's a goal you're striving toward. The intensity of your struggle will not last forever. It's a season that will pass. To help you look beyond it, you may wish to develop a list of the qualities you're working to possess. In my case, I wanted to be courageous, confident, and uncompromising. As you move forward, remember that hope is a choice, a gift, and a virtue. It's not a mood. You must choose it, ask God for it, and work to develop it.

As you progress in your healing, consider how many lives you can touch on the way. Realize the power of your voice not only to stop abusers but to help victims of abuse to stop living out of their wounds. Depending on what you have been through, some people might hold it against you. But don't worry about them. If people are so obsessed with defining you by your past that they can't see who you have become today, they don't deserve to be a part of your future. As I once heard, "No matter how dirty your past is, your future is still spotless."

Have you ever noticed that bad habits are easily formed and difficult to break, whereas good ones are hard to develop and easily broken? If you've seen this pattern in your life, you're not alone. If you think lasting change is impossible because your efforts always seem to fall short, don't abandon your resolutions. Instead, take a deeper look at your approach. You were perhaps focusing on the fruit of the problem rather than looking at the root. Looking at life this way requires more effort because we invite our intellects to chaperone our emotions; we let our heads guide our hearts.

We also sometimes mistakenly think that our vices are part of our personalities. For example, I used to believe that my anger and lack of self-control were simply part of who I am. Because these traits had been a part of my personality for so long, I figured they were aspects of my temperament. The reality was that the flaws were rooted in unresolved hurts. Lasting change occurred within me only when those hurts began to be addressed.

What we need to realize is that forgiveness is not a feeling. It's a choice. It's a decision to wish mercy upon another instead of harm. Forgiving someone does not mean that the person shouldn't be brought to justice. A guilty person should be brought to justice. Forgiving *does* mean that we let go of our craving for vengeance and retaliation. We might be tempted to wish harm on the person who harmed us, but by refusing to forgive, we do not bring any harm to the other; we only punish ourselves. If you feel incapable of forgiving others, pray for the gift of a merciful heart, and remember that forgiveness is not a sign that the offense was unimportant. On the contrary, it's a sign that mercy is powerful and that love is stronger than hate. Forgiveness often requires heroic virtue—especially when we need to forgive ourselves. In my case, this took more time and effort than forgiving my abusers.

We have a Savior Who took on our humanity to take on our shame. We have a God Who knows the pain of betrayal, abandonment, humiliation, and violence, Who shows us that wounds can be healed and can be purified. It's okay if your past is messy. Sometimes, the process of healing is messy as well. Just look at the Gospels: Jesus sometimes used mud and spit to cure people. Perhaps He wanted to communicate that He's not afraid of the mess.

At one time in my life, I struggled with relating to Jesus as a man because men had hurt me many times. But because His Presence was veiled in the Eucharist, I approached Him without this obstacle between us. When you know someone loves you, you trust that person. The same is true in our relationship with God.

When we trust Him, we begin to practice the most powerful virtue in the world: obedience. This word is often viewed negatively and equated with submission. But in reality, it is the key that unlocks a vault of limitless graces.

No matter what your future may be, now is not meant to be a time of waiting. Instead, God is teaching you something each step along the way, preparing you to take His hand and walk with Him, trusting that God will lead you to healing.

If you're unsure how to begin the process of healing, here are the four pillars that supported my restoration process:

1. Find a Catholic counselor and be transparent about everything you've experienced.
2. Find a good priest for Confession and spiritual direction—a priest to whom you can be accountable.
3. Spend time in Eucharistic adoration, especially after your counseling sessions, taking time to process through prayer and journaling what you learned. This has transformed me as a woman. St. John Paul II said, "In that little host is the solution to all the problems of the world."
4. Remove toxic people from your life and replace them with those who will surround you with love and support.

I found that by doing these four things consistently, I made more progress in a short period than I had in years of attempting all sorts of other solutions.

You have God's light and gifts and a powerful love to offer. Don't be afraid that your scars will obscure the light. You might feel as if your life has been irreparably shattered, but consider this: when you bring shards of glass together and shine radiant light through them, you create stained glass. Likewise, God can bring beauty through our scars. He can turn us into living cathedrals. All we need to do is trust in His promise: "Behold, I make all things new" (Rev. 21:5).

If you have a
problem in your
life that you
can't fathom or
understand, you
have to examine
your prayer life,
not the problem.

MOTHER ANGELICA

SPACE FOR GRACE

Dr. Kymberly Scipione

M y therapeutic journey began thirty years ago, during one of the darkest moments of my life. I was a freshman in college and had just moved to a new state where I didn't know anyone. I had lived in a dorm for only about six weeks when this traumatic, life-changing event happened.

Isolated from all the comforts and supports I once had, I didn't know in whom to confide. Although I had already made some new friends, those relationships were not at a stage at which I could be vulnerable and ask for comfort in my state of crisis. And because of the shame I felt from my recent trauma, I didn't think it was an option to call home for help. It didn't seem like something I could disclose over the phone. Although my fourteen-year-old sister was my best friend, I didn't want to burden her with my situation. So I hid.

Days passed as I lay in my small twin bed; I left my dorm only to attend classes, and then I returned and crawled back into my bed. I lost my appetite as well as any motivation to make a trip to the dining hall. In the darkness of my solitude, a terrifying anxiety swept over me, and an inescapable cloud of depression seemed to hover above me. My feelings of worthlessness and inadequacy, compounded by my inability to erase the pain, caused me to begin fantasizing about falling asleep and never waking up. Granted, some friends would knock on the door to check on me, but I didn't answer. My roommate also decided it was best to stay away and let me be. I had joined a sorority but told them I was homesick, and that seemed to excuse my lack of involvement.

Eventually, I shared the story of my trauma with them, and amid a room full of tears, I was met with hugs and support. However, when you are in such a deep state of shame, isolation sometimes feels like more of a comfort (even though the opposite is the best medicine). After five nights of little sleep and many tears, I gathered enough strength to go to the Catholic campus ministry church at the Newman Center. I approached the priest and probably looked like an absolute mess with my tangled hair, disheveled clothes, and lack of basic hygiene! Taking one look at me and seeing the tears streaming down my face, he approached me with a hug and offered me a place to sit.

For the first time since the event, I felt safe and not alone. I am not sure how many hours he sat with me, simply offering me a space to grieve. Although I probably didn't make much sense between my sobbing, shaking, and talking, I never felt like an inconvenience or a burden to him. While assuring me of his support, he offered to call a religious sister who could offer me female encouragement as well. Immediately, Sr. Catherine arrived and listened to my story. For the first time, I felt hope as my shame began to lift. After this initial visit, she and I began to meet weekly to continue the healing journey together.

Although I don't remember each of the wonderful moments with Sr. Catherine, I'll never forget when she told me, "You are a victim of society, and God will hold you close." When she first said this, I didn't like hearing it. It made me feel as if I had no control over my life. But as time progressed, we talked through what this meant for me. She encouraged me to look at my life, to consider with whom I was surrounding myself, and to think about the decisions I needed to make moving forward. She reminded me that

I had complete control over these things, and that if I listened to God, He would be there to guide me on my journey.

For me to accept this, however, I needed to sort through the anger I felt toward God for not protecting me in those moments. Through Sr. Catherine's counsel, I was able to discover that no matter how alone I felt in those darkest of moments, God never left my side. Sr. Catherine gave me the freedom to feel what I was feeling, the time to grieve with her, and the space to feel loved and safe in the world again. I'm deeply grateful for her, as she renewed my faith in goodness and in Christ.

It was through her compassion that I was able to realize that I could use this life experience to help others. Gradually, my anger was transformed into empathy for others. The burden became a gift. In order to use this life lesson for the good of others, I volunteered at the clinic on campus and changed my major to psychology and sociology.

Now, many years later, I've worked professionally in residential treatment centers, community mental health centers, schools, and private practice. I've worked with women who have been through horrific experiences, and I've seen how those who heal from such events become powerful.

But counseling services aren't only for those who have experienced profound trauma. Life has become more stressful and less predictable for everyone, and as a result, the need for mental health support is greater than before. For example, many of my clients feel isolated and alone, even in a house full of children. They are the ones who give everyone in their homes room to feel anxious, depressed, or angry while not being given such room themselves.

If you feel that you might benefit from therapy, where can you find help? Step one is to know what you're looking for. The most important aspect of a good therapeutic relationship is to find a professional you can trust and feel safe with. Typically, within the first thirty minutes of meeting with a therapist, there will either be a sense of connection or not. If you don't feel such a connection, this is nothing against you or the therapist; rather, it is a sign that the two of you might not be a good fit. Therefore, give yourself the freedom to continue the search for the right person. Look for someone you can relate to, someone with whom you share similarities.

When I seek therapy (yes, good therapists go to therapy too), I prefer someone who has a background similar to mine; for example, someone who is educated, married, and has a larger family. I have five children and have felt judged by colleagues who think that is too many or that I should be at home instead of having a private practice. Managing a marriage, a family, and a career can be overwhelming, and therefore I prefer someone who can relate to these challenges. As a Catholic, I also search for Catholic therapists who can integrate our Faith into the healing process.

Inquire and interview mental health professionals about their credentials, training, and beliefs of the therapeutic process (in some states, people who have no formal training can call themselves therapists). Know what your needs or goals are. If your history includes trauma, you want a person who is trained in trauma and a scientific, research-based model. Two models that are the most researched and get the best outcomes are Eye Movement Desensitization and Reprocessing (EMDR) and Internal Family Systems (IFS). They also align with Catholic values, as they honor and encourage faith for healing.

If you find a Catholic therapist whom you can relate to and trust and who knows how to use these models of healing, that's a positive start. But don't stop there. Interview therapists to assess how well trained they are with EMDR and IFS. Are they certified EMDR consultants with EMDRIA (the professional organization that credentials EMDR therapists), or did they simply take a weekend course? Do they have a weekend of experience or years of training and thousands of hours of clinical therapy and clinical supervision? This can make the difference in the outcome of the work.

Once you have found the right fit and established a therapeutic relationship with a professional, the work can begin. Allow three to six sessions to establish trust and to arrive at the point where the deeper healing can begin. Because our bodies and our minds create defense mechanisms, it requires time to feel safe and process life events. Often, intensive work with EMDR or IFS, or both, will be less effective if it begins before the client feels safe enough to trust the counselor deeply.

I often think that my job title should be "Secret Keeper," as that is the best descriptor of what I do. My task is to hold space for secrets, allowing individuals to be safe and free of judgment. Because it is natural to fear the judgment of others, our nervous system can feel "off" when we're asked to be vulnerable with a stranger. Time alone allows our defense mechanisms to relax so that we can be free to access our authentic selves and discover things about them. If you are married, it also helps if your spouse is willing to get to know your counselor. When individuals are nurtured and supported by their spouses, they tend to have more positive outcomes in healing. A husband's behaviors that trigger negative reactions in his wife can be adjusted so that his interactions with her can provide her with moments of safe vulnerability. As a result, the entire family becomes healthier.

My own therapeutic journey began in the fall of 1990 and continues today. There are still moments where I feel triggered, and when this happens, I have learned to take note of it and check in with my psychologist for support. There is no shame in experiencing a trigger when you give yourself the freedom to explore what it's revealing to you. When I handle my difficult moments this way, my family doesn't become the dumping ground of my past traumas. Instead of transferring the hurt to them, I transform it.

Although the process of seeking support might seem intimidating at first, don't allow this fear to prevent you from beginning your healing journey. In time, your fear of vulnerability can be transformed into an experience of true empowerment.

> *Prayer to St. Joan of Arc*
> In the face of your enemies,
> in the face of harassment,
> ridicule, and doubt,
> you held firm in your faith.
> Even in your abandonment,
> alone and without friends,
> you held firm in your faith.
> I pray that I may be as bold
> in my beliefs as you, St. Joan.
> I ask that you ride alongside me
> in my own battles.
> Help me be mindful that
> what is worthwhile can be won
> when I persist.
> Help me hold firm in my faith.
> Help me believe in my ability
> to act well and wisely.
> Amen.

Sometimes
disappointment is
an opportunity to
grow in holiness.

MOTHER ANGELICA

CHAPTER 9

HE'S LYING TO YOU

Cameron Fradd

When [Satan] lies, he speaks
according to his own nature, for he
is a liar and the father of lies.

JOHN 8:44

Yep, it's true—he's lying to you. Now, don't get me wrong. I'm not talking about some man in your life or a politician or the media. I'm talking about Satan, aka the "father of lies." What's more, he has been lying to women since the beginning. Remember Eve? It all started when he lied to her, and she believed him. He told her that God wasn't telling her the truth or looking out for her, so God couldn't be trusted. What he really meant was that God didn't love her after all.

He lied to Eve, but is he also lying to you? Believe me, if you've got a pulse, then Satan is lying to you. It's the way he operates. "The devil prowls around like a roaring lion, seeking some one to devour" (1 Pet. 5:8). You have immeasurable dignity and worth, and you are deeply loved by the Father. Satan wants nothing more than to convince you otherwise.

Some of the lies Satan tells are unique to each of us. But after years of talking to women and listening to their hearts, I've come to believe that many of the lies he speaks are very similar:

117

"YOU'RE NOT BEAUTIFUL."

"YOU'RE STUPID."

"YOU'RE A DISAPPOINTMENT."

"YOU'RE TOO MUCH FOR PEOPLE."

"YOU'VE MADE TOO MANY MISTAKES."

"YOU DON'T DESERVE LOVE."

I could go on.

When we start to believe what Satan is telling us, it's much more tempting to sin. Eve believed the lies that Satan told her and acted on that belief. *Then destruction and pain followed.*

That's pretty much where I found myself one night in my teen years: rock bottom. Years of stress were wearing on me, and I was deep in self-hatred and destructive behavior. And there was anger—lots and lots of anger. My mom and I were constantly fighting. I just had a messy breakup with my boyfriend, and my friends blamed me for the fallout. I remember thinking, "I'm done. I'm just done." I felt numb and full of despair. "IT WOULD BE EASIER TO JUST END IT. THERE WOULD BE SUCH RELIEF," said the liar.

"She shall crush his head." (see Gen. 3:15)

My saving grace all those years was my relationship with our Blessed Mother, Mary. As a teenager, I felt as if I couldn't talk to Jesus because I was too sinful and too messed up. Jesus felt off-limits. "JESUS DOESN'T WANT TO TALK TO SOMEONE LIKE YOU," said the liar.

But it was a different story when it came to the Blessed Mother. It was easy for me to talk to our Lady. She is such a loving mother. I could easily picture her standing in front of me when I talked to her.

The beautiful thing about Mary is that she always points us to her Son. In fact, one dark autumn night—when I was despairing and at rock bottom—that's exactly what she did for me. Alone in the bathroom, scared by my desperate circumstances, I found the courage to cry out to Jesus: "Help me!" In my mind's eye, I saw the Blessed Mother step aside, and there, waiting to save me, was Jesus. That's all I remember of that night, but the months that followed were filled with miracles of emotional healing.

That January, I went with my youth group to a large weekend retreat. On Saturday night, we all gathered as a group to pray and praise the Lord. My friends were having powerful Holy Spirit experiences all around me. I felt awkward and uncomfortable, so I went to the back of the room to be alone. All of a sudden, I was flooded with feelings of guilt over mistakes I had made. I remember being really upset and overwhelmed with pain, and I just didn't like myself at all. I was replaying all of my past in my head. "REMEMBER WHAT YOU'VE DONE. THERE'S NO HOPE FOR YOU," said the liar.

Then, in the middle of this awfulness, I remember feeling a woman's hand on my shoulder. I assumed it was one of the adults who were helping out. It was so comforting to have her hand there that I reached up and put my hand on hers, and I just rocked from side to side, crying for the first time in forever. I began to feel as if everything was going to be okay and that I didn't have to feel all the pain anymore.

A friend came to check on me since she noticed I had looked upset when I went to the back of the room. She invited a priest to come over and pray with me, and the next thing I knew, I was lying on the ground, and I couldn't get up. It was as if the Holy Spirit rushed over me, and when I surrendered to God, I was filled with such peace! As the priest prayed over me, I felt pressure on my forehead, my chest, and my shoulders. It wasn't until years later that I realized those pressure points were in the shape of the cross.

When the priest finished praying, my friend encouraged me to go to Confession. It was my first really good Confession. God's mercy is so abundant! I left the confessional feeling completely free! There are no other words to describe it. I just felt free! In an instant, the despair I had been feeling was gone, by God's grace. I know that's not usual, but it really changed instantly. I wasn't depressed anymore! I still had some anger and self-hatred to work through, but nothing like before.

I left the confessional and went to look for one of our chaperones. I found one and asked, "Where's the lady who came up behind me and had her hand on my shoulder when I was crying? I want to thank her." He looked at me, confused. "Cameron, I was watching the whole time to make sure you were okay, and there was no woman behind you."

My inner healing took a huge leap that night, and the rest was to come in the following years. There were still lies to be exposed.

"You will know the truth,
and the truth will make you free." (John 8:32)

Going to youth group led me to join a youth ministry called NET Ministries. The Lord knows I love adventure, and NET completely fit the bill. I spent a few years traveling with a team of Catholic missionaries, leading retreats for teenagers. Although I loved leading retreats for teens and sharing the Gospel with so many people, I'm most grateful for the fellowship of the other women on my team. They were able to love me in my messiness, and they stood by me as I worked to identify other lies in my heart.

I was such a work in progress—and I still am! Having on my team these beautiful ladies who loved me and challenged me in my lies absolutely changed me. Have you ever heard the expression "God loves you the way you are but loves you too much to leave you that way"? I think the same is true of some holy friends who love you. I came to realize in high school and in my youth group that

I was wearing a mask. I was trying to present myself in a certain way, but I don't think anyone realized it until I lived in such close relationship with the women on my team.

I was having a long conversation with my team's supervisor one day. God knew what He was doing when He paired us together. Lynn was quiet and rock solid. She told me, "When I was younger, people used to assume that I didn't like how I looked and that I had low self-esteem. People see you, Cameron, and they think you have great self-esteem."

I immediately launched into thanks: "Aw, thanks, Lynn! I really appreciate that!"

But she wasn't finished. "Well, the truth of the matter is that I actually have great self-esteem, even though people don't think that I do. I know exactly who I am and Whose I am. And I don't think I've ever met anyone with lower self-esteem than you, Cameron."

Ugh—knife to the heart! It leveled me. In one sentence, I realized my mask wasn't working. I thought I was safe behind it, but Lynn saw right through it. What she said might sound harsh, but you have to know the love with which she said it. I knew Lynn loved me, and her persistence in pursuing me proved it. I was challenging to deal with, but Lynn and my teammates were relentless in their love for me. When you have that kind of security net, you can be more fearless in taking off your mask and getting real with the lies that you believe about yourself.

One of the lies I believed was that my personality was too much for people to handle and too much for the Lord. I remember being in prayer one day, basically having an argument with God. "Why did you make me 'too much'?" I demanded. Some of the women on my team were so calm and quiet, and I felt like the complete opposite. "HOLINESS DOESN'T LOOK LIKE YOU. IT LOOKS LIKE A HOLY CARD," said the liar. I was sure that holiness could never look and sound like me. The temptation was to think that I just wasn't made right.

And yet time and again, the women on my team would love me in my worst moments, and that love would challenge the lie. In the middle of that argument I was having with God, one of my teammates walked into the bedroom we shared. Not one to hold back my feelings, I barked at her to get out. After I calmed down, I went to find her to apologize.

"It's okay," she smiled. "I knew you weren't mad at me and that you were talking to God and were mad at Him." Love is such a healing force.

The women on the team were committed to loving me, and their loyalty gave me the courage to challenge the lie. "These women are sticking by me. Maybe I'm not too much after all," I dared to think. That created an opening in my heart to ask the Lord, "God, I feel like I'm too much, but am I really?" Then He slowly, gently revealed to me how precious I am in His eyes.

"The unfolding of thy words gives light." (Ps. 119:130)
Over the course of my time with NET, Lynn encouraged me to write down on index cards the lies I had believed about myself. I was to take the lies to prayer and ask God what the truth was. On the back of the index cards, I wrote Scripture passages I found that combated the lies. It was a heart-changing experience.

God also gave me examples that challenged the lies and inspired me. There were other women in the ministry with full, exuberant personalities who seemed so free and at peace with themselves. One of them would do cartwheels in the snow with complete abandon! She seemed so at peace with her full-throttle approach to life. Then the Lord introduced me to St. Joan of Arc, who immediately grabbed my attention. Here was a saint after my own heart: fearless, driven, headstrong! These kinds of women challenged the lie in my heart that holiness had to look a certain way.

"He set me free in the open ... because he loves me." (see Ps. 18:19)
For so long, I was at war with myself because of this lie of being "too much." It made me hide my heart from friends. I was always scared to share with my teammates what was really going on within me. I thought that my burdens were too heavy to share and that the weight of them would crush these women if they knew what was really in my heart. "IF THEY KNEW THE REAL YOU, THEY WOULDN'T LOVE YOU," said the liar. We would have times of sharing, and I would always go last, desperately hoping that time would run out and they'd have to skip my turn. But then I would share, and they would love me anyway.

You might wonder what makes these lies so destructive. For one, they're exhausting. We end up spending so much energy trying to hide what we think is a problem with the way we were made. We end up acting out of the lie rather than letting the truth of who we are animate us and our choices. Lies cause us to put distance between us and God. And that's never good.

The truth is that God loves us passionately and has given us His Holy Spirit. He has given us a spirit of power, love, and self-control (see 2 Tim. 1:7). We have an anointing on our lives as baptized women of God, and we have a mission to be salt and light in the world. When we believe this with all our heart, we live differently. The truth sets us free to love and be loved. We're all made differently, but we're made as lovely as the lilies of the field (see Song of Sol. 2:1–2).

Think about the statues and pictures of the Blessed Mother that you've seen. She's often shown standing on the head of the serpent from the Genesis story. Eve let the serpent whisper in her ear, but

Mary puts him far from her ear—under her heel, to be exact. Mary doesn't listen to lies, because she has fully embraced the truth of God's love for her. There's no room for lies in her heart. We can ask Mary to help us to be more like her in embracing the truth.

When you find yourself hiding, stressed, anxious, angry, or feeling any other negative emotion, ask yourself: "What's behind this feeling? Am I feeling this way because a belief in my heart is causing it? What am I believing, and am I sure it's true? Is it causing me to make poor choices and to sin? Is it causing some self-destructive behavior? Does it feel as if I'm throwing my lie in other people's faces?" These are signs there may be a lie in our hearts somewhere and that it's messing with us.

Shine a Light on It

My advice for battling a lie is to shine a light on it. What do I mean? Tell your struggle to someone you trust and whose faith you admire. Satan loves darkness and secrecy when it comes to lies, and simply speaking it out with someone wise and faithful can bring a ton of clarity.

Sometimes the lies we believe really seem true. I believed in lies for a very long time. But they caused me so much pain. Sharing with someone I trusted helped open my eyes to the truth.

Also, don't forget the healing power of the sacrament of Confession. Now that we are armed with this knowledge of Satan's tactics, we might be tempted to brush aside our consciences, telling ourselves that *any* negative feelings are just Satan's lies. A good confessor can help us discern the difference between a lie and a (rightfully) guilty conscience. Receiving the sacrament of Confession regularly is a great way to make sure we aren't justifying our sinful behavior. God's mercy is endless!

Another good test is to do what my supervisor, Lynn, had me do. Test the belief against God's Word. In a quiet place, ask the Holy Spirit to help you. With a stack of index cards in hand, write in pencil what you believe about yourself on one side of a card. Then do a prayerful search for what God is saying to you about that topic in Scripture. Flip the card over and write in permanent ink what the Lord is telling you. That's what I did. I've listed some common lies and some Scripture passages that address them at the end of the chapter.

Does any of this ring true for you? If so, know that you're not alone. You might think you'll never get through your struggle to see yourself as God sees you. You might think your struggle will last forever, but you *will* get through it. The Blessed Mother has her hand on your shoulder, no matter where you are, and God is relentless in His pursuit of you. You might feel like that one sheep who just can't get her act together compared with the ninety-nine. Fear not. Jesus is coming for you.

The Lie	The Truth
I've messed up and am no good.	If any one is in Christ, he is a new creation; the old has passed away, behold, the new has come. (2 Cor. 5:17)
I'm not beautiful.	You are all fair, my love; there is no flaw in you. (Song of Sol. 4:7)
I'm not pure.	Do you not know that you are God's temple and that God's Spirit dwells in you? (1 Cor. 3:16)

I'm not lovable.	See what love the Father has given us, that we should be called children of God. (1 John 3:1)
I'm not worthy of marriage.	I know the plans I have for you, says the LORD, plans for welfare and not for evil, to give you a future and a hope. (Jer. 29:11)
I can do it myself. I don't need anyone.	But we have this treasure in earthen vessels, to show that the transcendent power belongs to God and not to us. (2 Cor. 4:7)
Denial doesn't hurt. It's easier than facing the truth.	Strive even to the death for the truth, and the Lord God will fight for you. (Sir. 4:28)
I'm not as special as others.	I have called you by name, you are mine.... You are precious in my eyes, and honored, and I love you. (Isa. 43:1, 4)
I'm supposed to have it all together.	Like the clay in the potter's hand, so are you in my hand. (Jer. 18:6)

We need to focus
on the gift of
Knowledge filling
our memory,
the gift of
Understanding
filling our intellect,
the gift of Love
filling our will.

MOTHER ANGELICA

CHAPTER 11

THE FEMININE GENIUS

Lisa Cotter

I cringed the first time someone told me that Pope St. John Paul II taught about a woman's "feminine genius." "Oh great, here we go again," I thought. "Just another way for the Church to try to make women feel *special*." Having grown up in the 1980s and '90s, I was a bit averse to anything that seemed to differentiate men from women. When I was a kid, the world repeatedly told me that *anything a guy could do, I could do it better*. With that mantra etched in stone, I was not about to let the Church use cutesy phrases to convince me otherwise. My assumption was that in using this phrase, John Paul II was trying to appease women for being restricted from the Church's hierarchy by letting them know how much everyone appreciates the casseroles we make for church potlucks. Little did I know that casseroles were the last thing on the pope's mind.[8]

In the late '80s and early '90s, an emphasis on women surfaced in Pope St. John Paul II's public addresses and writings. During this period, he published an encyclical on Mary, titled *Redemptoris Mater* (*Mother of the Redeemer*), and an apostolic letter on the role of women, titled *Mulieris Dignitatem* (*On the Dignity and Vocation of Women*). Additionally, in 1995 he taught monthly, sometimes even weekly, on the topic of women during his public addresses.

[8] See my book *Reveal the Gift: Living the Feminine Genius* (West Chester, PA: Ascension Press, 2022)

129

Finally, smack-dab in the middle of that year, he wrote his much-loved *Letter to Women*. From all these sources arose a treasury of insights on women's unique nature, which he referred to as the "genius of woman" or the "feminine genius."

His aim in each of these efforts was not to put femininity into a neat little box. Instead, when the world was pushing women to become more like men, John Paul II sought to draw out the beauty of women's unique genius. This genius was so important to him that he called it "vitally essential to both society and the Church."[9]

Vitally essential. Those are some strong words from our beloved pope. He did not write them as a nice way to affirm women. He wrote them because he believed that understanding, appreciating, and cultivating this genius was critical for fully understanding both women and men.

Complementarity

In his *Letter to Women,* Pope St. John Paul II wrote, "It is only through the duality of the 'masculine' and the 'feminine' that the 'human' finds full realization."[10] To put it simply, men and women make sense only in light of each other. This concept, which the pope called "complementarity," is visible in basic biology, as the structure of a man's body makes sense only in light of a woman's body, and vice versa. Thus, when man and woman come together in sex, they complement, or complete, each other.

---

[9] Pope John Paul II, Angelus, July 23, 1995, in *John Paul II Speaks on Women*, ed. Brooke Williams Deely (Washington, D.C.: Catholic University of America Press, 2014), no. 2.

[10] Pope John Paul II, *Letter to Women* (June 29, 1995), no. 7.

Yet this complementarity is not limited to sex. In the abstract, men and women complement each other by using their gifts, talents, and strengths in uniquely masculine and feminine forms.

Affirming Pope St. John Paul II's assessment, Pope Francis declared, "When we treat a problem among men we arrive at a conclusion, but if we treat the same problem among women, the conclusion will be different: it will go on the same road, but it will be richer, stronger, more intuitive."[11] Whether it be a church, family, work, or political setting, when men and women bring their different strengths to the table, a more complete picture is drawn.

What Is the Feminine Genius?

Although Pope St. John Paul II is known for his teachings on the feminine genius, he never gives a concrete definition of the concept in his works. Instead, he asks us to "reflect carefully on what it means to speak of the '*genius of women*.'"[12] Many have answered this call, and their insights greatly contribute to the conversation. However, I am quite partial to one woman's thoughts, those of Sr. Prudence Allen, R.S.M.

Sr. Prudence has devoted decades to the study of womanhood. Her three-volume magnum opus, *The Concept of Woman*, is a treasure to the Church. In it, she defines the feminine genius as such: "The phrase 'genius of woman' refers to a way of being, acting, and

---

[11] Catholic News Agency, "Pope Francis Reminds Christians to Have a Festive Faith," Angelus News, May 16, 2015, https://angelus-news.com/news/us-world/pope-francis-reminds-christians-to-have-a-festive-faith/.

[12] Pope John Paul II, *Letter to Women*, no. 10.

loving in the world, which manifests a unique creativity in human relationships."[13]

According to Sr. Prudence, the feminine genius is not about *what* women have to offer the world; instead, it is about *who* God created them to be. It is about their essence, which is the same today as it was for the woman crossing the prairie in a covered wagon or the woman walking the dusty roads of Palestine during Jesus' earthly lifetime. A woman's genius, her way of "being, acting, and loving," does not change; what changes is the world in which she lives.

This genius is not about how smart or talented women are; instead, it is about the distinctive, feminine way women relate to others. This is critical because God did not create humans to be alone; He created them to live in relationships with others. According to Pope St. John Paul II, through relationships, women (and men) discover their purpose. As the pope wrote in his *Letter to Women*, "For in giving themselves to others each day women fulfill their deepest vocation."[14] It is in the giving of ourselves that we discover who we are.

In an effort to bring this all together, here is how I summed it up in my book *Reveal the Gift*: "The feminine genius is the *person-oriented disposition* of woman. It is the unique, feminine way women relate to humanity."[15]

With a working definition in place, it's time to return to the strengths of women.

---

[13] Sister Prudence Allen, RSM, *The Concept of Woman*, vol. 3, *The Search for Communion of Persons, 1500–2015* (Grand Rapids: William B. Eerdmans, 2016), 475.

[14] Pope John Paul II, *Letter to Women*, no. 12.

[15] Cotter, *Reveal the Gift*, 14.

Feminine Gifts

Although John Paul II never defined the "genius of woman," he emphasized several words when speaking on the topic. These words include receptivity, maternity, intuition, sensitivity, fidelity, generosity, strength, self-giving, beauty, humility, and more. It is critical to note that these strengths, or gifts, as John Paul II often referred to them, are not meant to be stereotypes. For example, when the pope highlights the unique sensitivity of women, he is not trying to reinforce the claim that all women are overly sensitive and cannot control their emotions. Exaggerated, overarching declarations like that are dangerous, as they place women in narrow parameters that do not fit every woman. Such parameters can make women feel less than they are. Although the gifts John Paul II highlights are *typical* of women, their *stereotypical interpretations* should never set the standards for authentic femininity. The way each woman expresses her feminine gifts varies widely, and that is a beautiful thing.

To affirm this idea, we need only look at the lives of female saints. Over the last two thousand years, the Church has canonized women who expressed their feminine genius in a myriad of ways. Some of these women were secluded, such as St. Thérèse of Lisieux, who never left her convent. Some were active, such as St. Teresa of Ávila, who founded convents all over Spain. Some were highly educated, such as St. Gianna Molla, who raised her children while practicing medicine. Some were uneducated, such as St. Joan of Arc, who bravely fought to save her country of France. Women saints who were young, old, single, married, religious, rich, poor, and of every race and tongue have been canonized by the Church. What elevated them was not their knowledge of Catholic trends or their ability to fit a current mold. It was the way they achieved holiness as they became who God created them to be.

In addition to these gifts not being stereotypes, they are also not exclusive to women. By highlighting the generosity or intuition of women, for instance, the pope does not imply that men are incapable of being generous or intuitive. Men, too, are called to cultivate and live these gifts in their own complementary, masculine way. This is because each of these gifts, or values, as Pope Emeritus Benedict XVI called them, are "above all human values."[16]

After writing beautifully on the gifts of women, Benedict explained it this way in his letter *On the Collaboration of Men and Women in the Church and in the World*: "It is appropriate however to recall that the feminine values mentioned here are above all human values.... It is only because women are more immediately attuned to these values that they are the reminder and the privileged sign of such values."[17]

To put it another way, because women tend to be more inclined to these gifts, they exemplify how to live them. It is their privilege to bring these gifts into the world and model them to the men in their lives, *who are also called to develop and live these gifts in complementary, masculine ways.*

With some key caveats in place, let us turn to two foundational feminine genius gifts: receptivity and maternity.

The Gift of Receptivity

In his *Theology of the Body*, Pope St. John Paul II wrote extensively on the deeper meaning of human sexuality. He explained that the structures of the male and female bodies are not a happy accident;

---

[16] Joseph Cardinal Ratzinger and Angelo Amato, *Letter to the Bishops of the Catholic Church on the Collaboration of Men and Women in the Church and in the World* (May 31, 2004), no. 14.

[17] Ibid.

rather, they reveal something about the vocation and nature of men and women.

In the marital embrace, the man's body gives, and the woman's body receives. While practical for procreation, this physical structure points to the profound truth that the body is a "visible sign of an invisible reality."[18]

When God created man and woman, He declared their creation—which included their physical bodies—to be "very good" (Gen. 1:31). The body is very good. Yet a human person is more than a body; he or she also has a soul. This body-soul composite is so closely connected that the body (a visible sign) reveals something about the soul (an invisible reality). In sex, a man's body gives in reflection of his soul, which God created to give in this world. A woman's body receives in reflection of her soul, which God created to receive in this world.[19]

For this reason, a woman's person-oriented genius tends to receive others into her heart. She opens herself up to people and searches for ways to meet needs, both physical needs and deeper, spiritual or emotional needs. She makes room for them on her calendar, at her table, and in her community. In doing so, she affirms the goodness, value, and dignity of each person she encounters.

The Gift of Maternity

Maternity is closely related to receptivity because the fruit of receptivity is maternity. To put it another way, a woman's ability to

---

[18] Pope John Paul II, General Audience, July 28, 1982, in *John Paul II Speaks on Women*, no. 5.

[19] This is not to say that only men can give and only women can receive. Both men and women are called to give and receive, yet because of a woman's receptive nature, she is the "privileged sign" of receiving.

receive is what makes it possible for her to mother. This concept is clearly visible in physical motherhood. But what about women who never become biological mothers? Are they still called to maternity?

Here again, a visible sign points to an invisible reality. Not every woman will bear a child physically, yet every woman has the space in her body to do so. Because God created her with this space, He also created her with the gifts and instincts needed to mother. This means that all women have the skills to "cherish, guard, protect, nourish and advance growth ... [in] all those in contact with her."[20] These skills, listed by St. Edith Stein, are not lying dormant, waiting for physical motherhood to take shape. Rather, every woman is called to live and express them—whether she is a physical mother or not.

This nonphysical expression of motherhood is what John Paul II called spiritual motherhood, and it is critical for our world. As John Paul II wrote in his *Letter to Women*, spiritual motherhood "has inestimable value for the development of individuals and the future of society."[21] This is because women, acting from their maternal genius, have the unique ability to "*acknowledge the person, because they see persons with their hearts.*"[22]

Women tend to see people as people, not as objects or things to be used for personal gain. They tend to recognize each individual's inherent dignity and value and desire to help others grow and develop into the persons they were created to be. Thus, John Paul II believed that "in a special way the human being is entrusted to woman, precisely because the woman in virtue of her special experience of

---

[20] Edith Stein, *Essays on Woman: The Collected Works of Edith Stein*, vol. 2 (Washington, D.C.: ICS Publications, 1996), chap. 1, "The Ethos of Women's Professions."

[21] Pope John Paul II, *Letter to Women*, no. 9.

[22] Ibid., no. 12.

motherhood is seen to have a *specific sensitivity* towards the human person and all that constitutes the individual's true welfare."[23]

Bringing It All Together

God entrusts humanity to women in a special way because of their receptive and maternal nature. *Women possess the capacity to receive and care for humanity.* How this capacity is manifested depends greatly on the call of each woman. Some carry it out in marriage and family life, others in their places of work or in the public sphere, others in their vocations to religious life, and still others in a combination of these settings. Wherever and however women express their feminine gifts, especially those of receptivity and maternity, they make the world more human.

If you have ever worried that you are not feminine enough for the Church, please wipe that thought from your mind right now. At its core, femininity is less about trends or stereotypes and more about how you love—how you receive and care for those entrusted to you. If that thought overwhelms you, be not afraid. From the beginning of time, God created every woman with the same person-oriented genius, so whether you feel like it or not, you have what it takes to be an authentic Catholic woman.

Know of my prayers, and be saints—it's worth it!

This chapter is based on my book Reveal the Gift: Living the Feminine Genius *from Ascension Press. I pulled out the most essential pieces, yet I could not cover everything that I wish I could. As a woman, what you have to offer this world is vital, and I*

[23] Pope John Paul II, post-synodal apostolic exhortation *Christifideles Laici* (December 30, 1988), no. 51.

sincerely want you to know how to live from it. For more on this topic, check out www.ascensionpress.com/revealthegift to grab a copy of the book, or connect with me at www.madetomagnify. com.

If you've got a
cross, carry it. It's
to make you holy.

MOTHER ANGELICA

CHAPTER 12

DIVORCE HURTS
MORE THAN TWO

Leila Miller

I magine two brides, each approaching her wedding day.

The first bride comes from an intact family, and she goes into her marriage with confidence of its permanence. She has no great anxiety or fear but simple joy at the thought of pronouncing her sacred promises before God and witnesses and with her family around her. She understands that in the years to come, there will be ups and downs, joys and sufferings, good times and bad, and even tragedies. She expects all of that, but she is not worried about the possibility of divorce or abandonment because marriage for life is a given. She knows in her heart, "We are in this till one of us dies. Till death do us part. *Period*."

The second bride is a child of divorce, and her thoughts and interior dispositions are entirely different from those of the first bride. She has anxiety, doubts, and an unspoken fear that she cannot shake. Even as every fiber of her being wants this marriage to be permanent (as permanence is marriage's nature), she is not sure how to get from here to there. She knows what her vows mean, and she means them sincerely, but she has no model to follow. The wedding itself, with her mother and stepfather on one side and her father and his third wife on the other, is a witness to the brokenness of her own foundation.

I was the "first bride." As a child of an intact family, I had no idea what a daughter of divorce faces in her marriage. Society never talks about it but only repeats the lines that "children of divorce are

141

resilient" and "children are happy when their parents are happy." So when I married my husband thirty-two years ago, I assumed that every woman approached her wedding in comfort and security, as I did. It was not until I was fifty years old and found myself doing unexpected research on the effects of divorce on children that the scales fell from my eyes. I suddenly saw the "great divide" that no one will address. I saw the world of millions of children of divorce, with common wounds, obstacles, and sufferings that are generally unknown to folks like me.

Many of you reading this are the "second bride." As a daughter of divorce, *your experience of your own marriage may be vastly different from the experience of a woman from an intact family.* The differences may be so profound that it can take a lifetime to unpack and explore, but let's not shy away from the discussion. Let's talk about the struggles that you face because of your parents' divorce. By looking at those wounds, often for the first time, you may find the beginning steps of healing for both yourself and your marriage.

First and foremost, please hear this: if you are a child of divorce having trouble in your marriage, you are not alone! It may not feel that way, though. In fact, when a daughter of divorce struggles with her marriage, she almost certainly feels isolated, believing that no one else is living through the same problems, trying desperately to cope. Because the culture in general does not acknowledge the serious and lifelong suffering of the children of divorce (and because the adult children of divorce who *do* try to speak out are instantly silenced), her own marriage is ripe for ongoing misunderstandings, a lack of communication, and feelings of loneliness. Those feelings can be especially acute if her husband came from a healthy, intact family.

Compounding the isolation is an unrealistic expectation that, despite coming from a broken home, a child of divorce should somehow be able to navigate marriage and parenting with competence and efficiency. Because the cultural narrative insists that divorce does not negatively affect children long term, this internal and external expectation of competence is a given, even though the children of divorce have not actually seen a model of normal, committed, healthy marital interactions growing up. The old adage that "we can't give what we don't have" comes into sharp focus for the child of divorce who is desperately trying to navigate marriage while blind to what a rightly ordered marriage should look like.

As one daughter of divorce told me: "We need to shed light on this specific topic because women like me know they have a problem but can't identify the problem. I know it took me a while to figure this one out, and I wish I'd had a resource to walk through the issues I struggle with in my marriage because of my parents' divorce. But the challenges of marriage for women like me was never brought up."

This "secret" is a huge weight and a potential threat to each of those marriages and families, which translates to a negative impact on society itself. After all, as St. John Paul II famously said, "The future of humanity passes by way of the family."[24] Healing families and safeguarding the next generations will require that the children of divorce figure out how to navigate marriage, working to ensure that any crooked paths are made straight.

To get to that healing, it is helpful to understand that there are experiences and effects that almost all children of divorce share. The similarities give a blueprint for what you, as a daughter of divorce, might encounter, and there are stages of realization of how your parents' divorce has affected you. We can call that process of realization "thawing out," and some children of divorce are further

---

[24] St. John Paul II, post-synodal apostolic exhortation *Familiaris Consortio* (November 22, 1981), no. 86.

along in that process than others. The younger you are, the more "thawing out" you have left to do, and in fact, you may not yet have realized how deeply your parents' divorce has affected you. The wound is primal, and it has robbed you of something that, by God's design, you were supposed to have.

We must speak plainly: the divorce was an injustice to you, the child. One or both of your parents sinned badly enough to deprive you of what God intended for you, something truly foundational for your life and for healthy functioning.

The sooner we admit that reality, the sooner understanding and healing can come—not so that you can accuse, berate, and resent the offending parent or parents but so that the truth will be known and your cross identified and so that you can move on from there in grace, forgiveness, and freedom. But without the basic knowledge of God's created order, and without an understanding of the truth of marriage permanence and the injustice of divorce, the soul is floating, unmoored, confused, chaotic, and vulnerable to familial and cultural gaslighting. Truth must come *first* before one can move on with clarity and purpose, confidently carrying the cross and receiving Christ's redemption and peace.

My friend LeeAnne Abel, a child of multiple divorces, has worked closely with hundreds of adult children of divorce over the years, helping them to "thaw out" and heal. Her work has revealed what most children of divorce have in common, which can be distilled into nine main categories:

1. Self-doubt, lack of confidence, insecurity, or anxiety
2. Anger
3. Difficulties with boundaries
4. Struggles with living out the Fourth Commandment (honoring one's parents)
5. Grief

6. Codependence
7. Loneliness
8. Difficulties with trust
9. Lack of tools for relationship skills

Although there isn't space in this chapter to discuss each of these issues in depth, they are worth exploring further, as it is important for a daughter of divorce to understand the main wounds that she will bring to her own marriage. If you would like to hear LeeAnne's fuller examination of each of these topics, please listen to her three-part podcast at RestoredMinistry.com:

Part 1: https://restoredministry.com/5

Part 2: https://restoredministry.com/6

Part 3: https://restoredministry.com/7

In the meantime, please know that the concerns and wounds you bear going into marriage—e.g., anxiety, doubt, insecurity, and even occasional paralyzing fear—are *normal* in light of your shattered foundation. Remember that God intended the remote preparation for marriage to begin in childhood. That preparation consists of a married father and mother rearing their children in love and stability. You never had that example or preparation. You are expected to function well in your own marriage while operating at a severe disadvantage.

Here's a clarifying analogy. Although everyone has struggles and difficulties in marriage, the adult children of divorce must handle the same issues while standing on a broken family foundation. It's as if the adult child of divorce is standing on an ice patch that breaks into two pieces beneath her feet. She may be able to keep herself standing upright, but there is a constant and considerable effort required to do so. Some adult children of divorce will end up falling, and even the ones who end up managing it well will suffer considerably in the process.

Some children of divorce not only have *two* separate families (pieces of ice), but with subsequent marriages and divorces by the parents, they experience a repeated breaking of the ice patch—two, four, six, or even more pieces that they must straddle precariously. Sometimes, it is impossible to keep hold of a piece that drifts away—that piece representing a stepparent, stepsiblings, or stepgrandparents who are set afloat with an additional divorce. Through these agonizing attempts at balance and survival, the world sees the survivors still standing somehow, and so they are thought to be resilient, coping well, and moving on uneventfully into their own marriages. That is often an illusion.

Navigating a broken family—standing atop those shattered ice patches—requires a lot of strength and a slew of coping mechanisms from the child of divorce. A background of pain, stuffing emotions, anxiety, distrust, disordered thinking, and growing up too soon (the parent-child relationship is often inverted in a divorce) intrudes on their own future marriages. Many of the coping mechanisms that seem to work with one's broken family of origin do *not* work when dealing with one's own marriage. The self-preservation measures necessary for the daughter of a broken family can be the very things that undermine the trust and security between spouses, and the "solutions" that a wife applies in her marriage, based on how she coped as a child, can be ineffective and even detrimental when dealing with her own husband. We see this when she tries to minimize problems, ignore conflict, or maintain a perfect façade—all of which last only for a time.

Many daughters of divorce suffer with feelings of unworthiness and lack of a firm identity. This can lead to contradictions. On the one hand, they may declare with everything they have that their children will never experience the pain of divorce, as they did, but on the other hand, and especially when there are disagreements with their husbands, they look for and entertain unconscious "exit ramps" from the marriage. One of the most destructive messages imparted to a child when parents divorce is that *problems are not resolved, and conflict leads to permanent separation.* That defective witness means that any conflict a daughter of divorce experiences in her own marriage may lead her to fear that the relationship is ending. Normal disagreements in marriage—which are not concerning to the children of intact families—can seem catastrophic when one does not have the skills or modeling from parents to overcome them. And because there is no gauge of "what is normal" gleaned from her family of origin, a wife may not be confident in knowing whether a loud or harsh word from her husband is within normal range or whether it's a calamity signaling the end.

A daughter of divorce may not know how to calibrate her anger and contempt in arguments, or she may go the other way and avoid any conflict whatsoever out of fear. She may also develop a stubborn independent streak that puts distance between her and her husband. Depending on her father's role in the divorce and what she witnessed, she may have absorbed the idea that men are untrustworthy, selfish, likely to cheat, and so forth. One particularly pernicious burden is when a daughter of divorce has a mother who harbors contempt for her ex-husband and expresses her disgust, anger, disappointment, and bitterness in front of her own children. The children are often conditioned to see their own spouses in the same light. "All men are [fill in the blank]!" or "Of course men are going to do that!" or "Don't expect anything more; he's just a man!" A wife's interactions with her own husband—*a man!*—can be heated and hostile because of this preconditioning from a divorced parent. Indeed, any trashing of one parent by the other is a detriment to the child. Because each parent is half of her own existence, the daughter of divorce suffers a great blow to her self-worth. The reality is that, in the divorce, "half of her" was cast off as unwanted, and the message received is that half of the adult child of divorce is unacceptable. Predictably, women with low self-worth (which is different from the virtue of humility) are less likely to have healthy marital interactions than those who are confident, have a strong sense of identity, and are at peace.

Many daughters of divorce come into their own marriages with "a past." The sad reality is that many of them, as teens or young adults from broken homes, had gone "looking for love in all the wrong places." This unchaste and even promiscuous behavior came from a longing for love, acceptance, and belonging to replace what had been lacking from one or both parents. Going down this dark path has led countless young women to accept poor treatment, lack of respect, and abuse in relationships, further solidifying their feelings of being worthless and being used by men. Later, as married women, they may feel self-loathing as they look back with regret on relationships they had when they were trying to cope with the devastation of their parents' divorce. Many daughters of divorce have also experienced the trauma of physical or sexual abuse, or both, inflicted by men whom their divorced mothers dated. Statistically, we know that biologically unrelated males pose a danger to young girls and teens in broken homes. A past of promiscuity or the trauma of sexual abuse by a mother's boyfriend or new husband can affect a woman's current marriage.

Married women with divorced parents often struggle with lack of confidence, self-doubt, insecurity, and anxiety, which were created (or greatly exacerbated) by years of trauma and often undergirded by limited attention and affirmation from their parents. The parents may not have intended the neglect, of course, but they themselves were going through the horrors of divorce and litigation, changes to their residences and standards of living, new romances or breakups, new marriages and families, and so forth. Some children watched one parent valiantly stand for the marriage vow as the other went on to start a new family, and often the children ignored or hid their pain, knowing how much the abandoned parent was suffering and not wanting to add to that.

Children naturally love their parents, and that is as it should be! When parents opt out of married life, however, roles can become reversed, and children can take too much on their young shoulders. The children of divorce do not want to add to the struggles and suffering of their parents even as they are told by one or both parents (and other adults in their lives) that the divorce was worth it because the parents are now "happy." Most children, no matter what their age at the time of parental divorce, are not free to express their confusion or their pain with their family members, and many never find that safe space at all.

A terrifying precedent for the children of divorce is watching a parent get kicked to the curb when that parent becomes unlovable. The clear message is that love is conditional: "I will love you so long as you please me. I will stay with you so long as you are lovable." Having received this message, imagine (as many of you can) the level of anxiety of a child of divorce going into her own marriage! The pressure to be perfect, never to let one's guard down, or never to have a bad day, week, month, or year is crushing and unsustainable. In fact, the entire concept of "I will love you only as long as you stay lovable" flies in the face of the marriage vow—and contradicts the witness of Christ, the true Bridegroom. After all, we don't need the marriage vow when times are good and the spouses are happy; we take the vow precisely for those times when we do *not* want to be married, when our spouses become "unlovable." The child of divorce has not seen that example of fidelity. She often doesn't have the tools to stay during hard times, nor does she feel confident that her husband will stay when she inevitably disappoints him.

Because of all this childhood baggage, daughters of divorce often live with the seemingly never-ending fear and anxiety that they will one day be abandoned. This ongoing worry causes unhealthy suspicions, lack of trust, lack of intimacy, and sometimes even the feeling that one needs to have a backup plan, just in case. One female contributor to my book *Primal Loss: The Now-Adult Children of Divorce Speak* describes it this way:

> For the first few years of my marriage, I was very on guard and prepared for my husband to leave. In fact, I expected it. Even though I knew he was a devout Catholic, I just thought that was what men did and that he would probably eventually decide to leave, even if it meant he'd be alone for the rest of his life. So, I would stash away money, hiding it in a drawer or my purse. I occasionally looked at the cost of efficiency or one-bedroom apartments; I would think about how things would be split up when he left. It wasn't that I wanted him to leave, but in my mind, it wasn't even a question of if it would happen but when it would happen. I didn't even realize at the time why I did those things, but now I know.

She realized after years of marriage that her fear of abandonment was an effect of her parents' divorce. She is far from alone. Another daughter of divorce told me this:

> The biggest effect [of my parents' divorce] overall is the constant lack of security I always feel. It's a sense of not having a safety net of sorts. The lack of security carries over into my own marriage. Like if my own father could betray my mother, me, and my sister, why is my own husband above

doing that? The bottom line is that my parents' divorce has brought insecurity into my own marriage. How could my husband love me enough never to betray our vows? Really, how is it even possible? I hate feeling that way.

Another woman told me the following:

> We have been married for nineteen years, and the beginning of our marriage was very difficult. As soon as I got married, I was sure my husband would cheat. I thought unless I could keep him perfectly happy, he would leave me. It seems bizarre to me today because he is such a good man, but it was really an honest fear. This led to so many fights, and I became so insecure and unhappy.

Many daughters of divorce feel that showing weakness, saying the wrong thing, or lacking skills that their absent parents never taught them will one day cause their husbands to leave. The pressure can be overwhelming and unrelenting, like waiting for the other shoe to drop.

One wife told me the following heartbreaking story, echoing the previous woman's concern about perfection:

> When I was a kid, I asked my dad why he and my mom got divorced. He said something like, "Oh, we argued about silly things, like who gets to use more of the blanket in bed and that sort of thing." I accepted that at the time, but as I got older, I realized his answer could mean one of two things:
>
> 1. People can get divorced over something as trivial as a blanket.
> 2. He didn't care about me enough to tell me the truth.
>
> I tend to believe #1, which means:

- My husband might leave me because I'm always so behind on laundry.
- My husband might leave me because I forgot to pack a lunch for him all week. (Note: He doesn't ask or expect this; I just do it because I like to. Still, I think if I don't go out of my way, he's outta here.)
- My husband might leave me because I suffer with depression, and while I'm usually able to manage it, there are times that I get pretty negative.
- My kids will be damaged by me.
- My kids will remember that "one thing" I said out of anger or sadness, and it will scar them forever.
- My kids will grow up well despite anything I have done, not because of it.

Basically, I feel as if I could lose my husband's love for something trivial.

Imagine living with that kind of anxiety in a marriage—both as a wife and as a mother! It becomes a recipe for unhappiness in marriage, and it can become a self-fulfilling prophecy.

Some women choose "independence" in a marriage as a protective measure. Here is what one such woman told me: "I have it in the back of my mind that things could all go wrong at any moment, and then I'd be on my own or a single mother. I feel like I have to be as independent as I can possibly be 'just in case.' It has made it more difficult for me to trust and even think long term."

Again and again, I heard the same themes from the daughters of divorce, even as each of them thought that *no one else* was thinking the same things or experiencing the same fears. Our cultural silence regarding the effects of divorce on children adds isolation and loneliness to the list of their sufferings.

With all that turmoil churning within the daughter of divorce, what of the husband's perspective? He is affected by his wife's broken childhood as well. A husband who comes from an intact family may be confused or dismayed by some of the dispositions of his wife and the struggles in his marriage. A daughter of divorce may have expectations about her childhood trauma being "all fixed" by entering her own marriage. The deeper the trauma she experienced, the higher the expectations she may have for her husband to heal it all. To be sure, the love of marriage *does* help set many things aright. However, a husband who does not come from a broken home will not likely understand his wife's profound wounds, and he will often not be the right audience for processing the trauma. It may be best for the wife to speak to a fellow daughter of divorce, one who is more "thawed out" than she and who has faced these issues already.

Certainly, she may share any insights with her husband. Also, having her husband's perspective of being from an intact home can be a real gift and example—not of perfection, but of how a normal, if imperfect, family functions. The spouses can truly be a gift to each other in this way, deepening their understanding of the importance and irreplaceability of a functioning marriage.

Of course, it also happens that two adult children of divorce marry each other. That shared experience can be helpful, although the spouses should make themselves very familiar with the common struggles of adult children of divorce so that those struggles do not harm their relationship. An understanding of right order and God's plan for marriage goes a long way, as do self-awareness, humility, and forgiveness. With prayer, virtue, and calling upon the grace of the sacrament of Matrimony, the spouses can break the spirit of divorce from *both* sides for the healing and flourishing of the next generations.

Issues outside the immediate home also tend to vex the adult children of divorce. One particularly common problem is the anxiety that surrounds important events. Harkening to that analogy of balancing on broken pieces of ice, a daughter of divorce may experience intense stress, almost to the point of decision paralysis, when planning events for holidays, weddings, Baptisms, graduations, children's recitals, and so forth. She feels the weight of the world on her shoulders, under pressure to invite the right combination of people, at the correct time and in the proper order, all to avoid hurting multiple people's feelings and causing conflict. It's an exhausting and nearly impossible task, and yet these occasions recur several times a year, for decades. This stress affects her current marriage each time, stealing her peace and distracting her from enjoying family celebrations with her husband and children.

Another outside trap that can snare a daughter of divorce comes, believe it or not, in the form of friends. One of the most devastating developments in our culture today is that women, who generally used to be marriage affirming, have too often become divorce affirming. Woman's innate tenderness and relational nature has been distorted and deformed, resulting in an overemphasis on empathy, feelings, and a misguided sense of compassion. Imagine a marriage-insecure daughter of divorce going to a group of friends for support in talking through the marital issues. Before the sexual revolution, she likely would have heard a balanced, reasonable viewpoint from her girlfriends, and they would have presented sound advice based on honor, virtue, and, yes, what is best for the children.

But now? In our therapeutic "me first" culture, she will likely be told to ditch the hard work of virtue, reject long-suffering, and go find her bliss—elsewhere. She will be told that she "doesn't deserve this," that "God wants her to be happy," and she may be advised to divorce, annul, and "move on." Her hope to provide her children with a stable home and to learn how to work through difficulties is too often met with dismissiveness by girlfriends who either do not have the skills or fortitude to work through marriage difficulties or who simply want to justify their own lack of commitment to their vows. As the *Catechism of the Catholic Church* (2385) says, divorce is contagious. The struggling wife will be invited into the circle of divorcées.

Here is what one daughter of divorce told me, describing a dinner with Catholic friends, one of whom had decided to divorce her husband and was announcing it to the others. The daughter of divorce, who had heard about her friend's intention earlier, had already told her friend privately that divorce would be devastating to her children and that she should stay married. Clearly, this is not the advice she got from the others:

One of the [Catholic ladies at dinner that night] informed the group that she was leaving her husband. She announced that she was a good mother and did not want to be judged. All of the women were supportive, affirming her, and being so kind to her. The conversation turned to how divorce affects the children, and immediately the same old lines were trotted out: the amazing resilience of kids, the idea that the happiness of the parents is crucial to kids' happiness, etc. And they all went on and on. What struck me, though, was that this group of eight Catholic women spoke with such authority, though they all came from intact homes. They said what was expected, what our friend wanted to hear. And that's how we do it; we give support instead of giving pushback.... To not go along is to judge and to be critical, and who wants to be that? So I sat there in silence because I realized that nobody was about to ask the one person in the room who had any direct experience with what it's really like being a kid going through divorce. No. We don't really want to get real. That's not what we do.

Ladies, please, pick your friends very carefully. Do not associate with divorce-affirming women. Your family, and even your soul, could depend on it. True friendship is based on virtue and on fidelity to the moral law and the teachings of Christ.

Are there times when extreme circumstances require a physical separation of spouses, even indefinitely? Yes, of course. And the Church, in her wisdom, has outlined what must happen in those sad cases, through Scripture, the *Catechism*, and canon law. The mind of the Church can be summed up in the words of Pope Leo XIII (emphasis mine): "When, indeed, matters have come to such a pitch that it seems impossible for [spouses] to live together any longer, then the Church allows them to live apart, and strives at the same time to soften the evils of this separation by such remedies and helps as are suited to their condition; *yet she never ceases to endeavor to bring about a reconciliation, and never despairs of doing so*."[25]

We must remember that only a small percentage of divorces occur because of high-conflict circumstances, such as violence, danger, mental torture, and the husband's starting a new family. We are conditioned to believe that these dire situations are the reasons people get divorced, but these types of heartbreaking cases are the outliers. In fact, most divorces are from low-conflict marriages. Every married couple includes two sinners, and oftentimes

---

[25] Pope Leo XIII, encyclical *Arcanum Divinae* (February 10, 1880), no. 41.

that reality leads to a souring of the marriage, a litany of bad habits and negative interactions, and just a general (but not dangerous) misery. At a certain point, a wife may become convinced that things are unfixable. However, a true friend can offer support and understanding while also encouraging self-reflection. If an adult child of divorce confides in a wise woman who offers perspective, guidance, and resources, a crisis can be averted, and the marriage can be healed. Rather than fuel the fires of a wife's discontent (which is all too easy), we women must do a better job of helping our struggling loved ones with resources, wisdom, and encouragement to save their marriages.

So much of the above can seem bleak, even hopeless. But if you are a child of divorce, do not despair! It was precisely for the broken of this world that the Lord came and offered Himself! "Those who are well have no need of a physician, but those who are sick" (Mark 2:17).

Christ came to set you free! Let's look at how the light can overcome the darkness.

A wife's self-reflection is crucial. Women are as prone to sin as men, and yet we have our blind spots. We often look at our husbands' sins and "helpfully" point those sins out to them, yet we tend to neglect the hard work of improving our own interior lives. By focusing on ourselves and examining the areas in which we lack virtue, we can better weather difficult times in our marriages. Of course, it is ideal that both spouses would work on themselves and the marriage, but a lot can be healed when even one spouse grows in virtue and becomes holy. No woman wants to think she can be controlling, critical, emasculating, ungrateful, disdainful, discontented, or contemptuous to the point that nothing her husband does can please her. But let's face it, ladies, most of us have work to do on ourselves in these areas.

A daughter of divorce (many of whom were raised by feminist mothers) might see only *his* weaknesses, *his* inabilities, *his* failures. She may be reticent to share her own vulnerabilities because she finds that too risky. In an attempt to protect her heart or avoid the necessary virtue of humility, or both, she may withhold from her husband her love, respect, affection, and admiration—which is the very oxygen men need! If a wife's parents made their marriage into a series of competitions and power plays in which someone must win and someone must lose, then she must learn a new dynamic.

Every healthy marriage operates on a steady stream of goodwill, and yet a child of divorce may never have seen patience, forgiveness, and reconciliation—i.e., goodwill—operative in a marriage before. If the opposite has been reinforced for so long, it is difficult for a wife to be gentle, feminine, and a "soft place to land" for her husband. Many daughters of divorce want to be competent, in control, independent, and even flawless, when what a husband needs to thrive is her God-given receptivity and femininity—a gift that she fears will make her look weak.

We know that Jesus is not only our Savior but our role model for how to live: we see Him serving and sacrificing for others, loving them through and despite their sin, and forgiving time and again. Yet fear, pride, and our fallen nature make those things hard and even burdensome for us. The world commands us to avoid the cross at all costs. Embracing the cross of a difficult marriage (or a difficult season of marriage) can seem foolish to a daughter of divorce who fears "I may end up with the short end of the stick when the marriage fails!" These negative, unholy messages can be a running loop in the back of her mind, but simply being *aware* that they are destructive and deceptive helps immensely. A child of divorce can find it hard to have hope during difficulties, but here is a wonderful, mysterious truth of our Catholic Faith: God uses suffering to help souls learn humility, lean on Him, and love better. Christian suffering, when offered in union with Christ's suffering, is redemptive. Understanding redemptive suffering is vital, as it gives meaning to our suffering and transforms it into a channel of grace for our and others' salvation.

God wants the marriage of a daughter of divorce to succeed and be sanctified. What can she do to cooperate with God's grace? One major key is to rightly order her emotions. *Emotions must always be subordinate to the intellect and the will.* Emotions can lead us astray, so they should never "lead" at all! A daughter of divorce can focus on maintaining intimacy and friendship with her husband even when she feels the desire to pull away. Like any new habit (and virtue is a habit), this will take time and effort. She can find friends who are marriage affirming and keep herself at a careful distance from those who would seek to drive a wedge between husband and wife, who are "one flesh" by Christ's decree. She can and must realize that even most priests, counselors, friends, or family members do not have the skills, knowledge, or faith formation to be truly helpful in dealing with a troubled marriage. She can seek mentors who *do* have those skills, knowledge, and faith formation, who understand how men and women are naturally different (a good thing!) and how the "marriage dance" works.

Through prayer and perseverance, a daughter of divorce can develop confidence in the goodness of both male and female parenting styles—a complementarity that God Himself designed. She can establish boundaries with any dysfunctional relatives from the family of origin, knowing that boundaries will help keep those relationships healthy and loving to whatever extent possible, so that the new and growing family can have pride of place and thrive. She can maintain the hope that problems that seem massive today may be calmed tomorrow, and she can recognize that marriage is a long-haul proposition: a lifelong space where sinners have the shelter and safety to be imperfect and to fall, receiving mercy and charity on the journey and never being discarded.

A daughter of divorce can reorient her past by leaving it in God's merciful hands and looking toward the future from the perspective of Heaven. She can see beyond the current difficulties in marriage to the hope of Christ's promises made possible by His grace: a beautiful, whole family of her own; no "moving on" to some new and shiny lie but, instead, the prospect of standing by her husband as her children, children's spouses, and grandchildren come home for Christmas—an intact extended family. She can paint that picture in her mind's eye, visualizing it often as a motivation.

Marriage is a life's work. If you are a daughter of divorce, you don't have to repeat your parents' mistakes. You are not destined to divorce because they did. You can make your own choices, grow in virtue, work out your marriage and your destiny with God—completely apart from the sins and decisions of your parents. Each and every daughter of divorce, who is first and foremost a daughter of God the Father, can seek and find the love and comfort of Mother Mary, the presence and glory of the Lord Jesus, the joy of the Holy Spirit, and the beauty and wisdom of the saints.

This brings us back to "bride one" and "bride two." It is true that the peace and joy of the first bride on her wedding day may not have been present for the second bride on hers. But that peace and joy are available to the second bride now and going forward. Armed with the knowledge of Christ's truth and the desire to grow in His virtue, each of us, whatever our origin, can conform ourselves and our futures to God's design, according to His holy will. Though the stories of our two brides have vastly different starting points, they can both end in happiness and holiness, rightly ordered through the astounding grace of a good and just God, Who has been with us, sometimes unseen, every step of the way.

Resources for children of divorce
RestoredMinistry.com
LifeGivingWounds.org
LeilaMiller.net/primallosspdf
LeilaMiller.net/secretfbgroups

Resources for marriage support
TheAlexanderHouse.org
Retrouvaille.org
LeilaMiller.net/marriagesupport
LeilaMiller.net/impossiblemarriagesredeemedpdf

Let us not be
confused by the
talents and mission
of other saints.
Let us be the kind
of saints we were
created to be.

MOTHER ANGELICA

CHAPTER 13

WE ARE WOMEN
AT THE WELL

Sarah Swafford

have always been fascinated with first-century Judaism and Christianity and the world that Christ journeyed through. There are so many aspects of that day that are vastly different from ours. There are also many things that are the same and that are at the root of the human experience and at the core of every human life, no matter what age a person is born into.

I love to ponder the women of the first century and what their day-to-day living, with all its chores, traditions, hardships, and joys, was like. I want to focus on one chore that seems to come up quite a bit in Scripture: the task of going to the well and drawing water for the day.

The women would go out early in the morning, before the heat and business of the day, to secure the water needed for their families. It was a strenuous task, but it was also somewhat of a social gathering of the community; the women would chat, catch up, and, I am sure, engage in a good amount of gossip.

Unlike us, they had no phone line, Internet connection, or social media to update them. No, it was in their comings and goings to places such as the well and the market and the Temple where they would interact and live life. And like us, those women struggled with some of the same things we struggle with — the doubts, fears, insecurities, loneliness, competition, pressure, and anxieties that can plague the human heart.

In my ministry over the years, I have noticed two questions that seem to come up often, not always asked out loud, but definitely in the minds and hearts of people I have walked with (and even in mine). Those two questions are "Am I enough?" and "Am I truly loved?"

We typically go on autopilot and don't really sit and ponder these two questions and their ramifications, but at the root of our struggles, those two nagging questions seem to linger.

When you think about first-century women and a well, your thoughts probably turn to the woman at the well in Samaria in St. John's Gospel (4:1–42). There are clues in the fourth chapter of the Gospel of John that point out more in the story of the woman at the well than we might at first notice. First, it says that it was "about the sixth hour," or about noon. Few women would choose the hottest time of the day to draw water, and this woman was by herself, which tells us that she was probably an outcast. Her reputation kept other women away, and she was not welcomed to be with them in the morning, or at least she must have felt that way.

It can be easy to look at her life and plight and feel as though you can't relate to her since she was on her sixth husband (John 4:18) and had quite the reputation in town. But when you look at her life and her story, it's easy to wonder: "What led her to that life of brokenness and sin?" Then it can be easy to relate to her. She, like so many of us, wrestled with the questions, "Am I enough?" and "Am I truly loved?" When you begin to doubt that you are enough and that you are truly loved (often at an early age), you start to make decisions and choices for your life based on those negative answers. If the answer to those questions is no, and you feel the emptiness of that no, you try to fill that space and overcome the ache that "you are not enough, and you are not *and will never be* truly loved." And that path can lead you down dark alleys where you never thought you would venture.

Whether it is the woman at the well, the other women of Samaria, or we women in the twenty-first century, one thing is true: Jesus' words at the well were meant for all of us. "Every one who drinks of this water will thirst again, but whoever drinks of the water that I shall give him will never thirst; the water that I shall give him will become in him a spring of water welling up to eternal life" (John 4:13–14).

We drag our heavy jars to the well every day; we throw them down into the dark well and fight to bring up water, only to drink it and be left unsatisfied. And so on we go, again and again and again, to that same well. Yes, we need water to live, but Jesus is driving at something much deeper here. Sit with this for a minute: *What do I "go to" when I feel like I am not enough and not truly loved? What do I put in my heavy jar and lug around, only to drink it and still feel unsatisfied?*

It can be many different things, and our jars will contain something different from others' jars, but countless people play (and have played over the centuries) the game of "I will be happy *if and when* ..." And we lug heavy jars filled with useless water back and forth from our homes every day. But Jesus says to you and me: "I want to give you water that will make you never thirst again—the water of eternal life."

Jesus is sitting next to the well, asking you, begging you: "Can I have your jar? It's heavy, and you don't need to carry it around anymore." It can be so easy to avoid our Lord with distractions, excuses, reasons that we are "fine, good, great, and busy, but still supposedly *good!*" But Jesus *sees* us, and He sees the ways that we dodge His love and gaze because of our feelings of unworthiness, our deep feelings of inadequacy.

Too often, we want to get our lives "together" and feel as if we are presenting the "best" or "perfect" versions of ourselves to others, and even to our Lord.

Years ago, I had a profound experience in Confession with a priest who loved me enough to point this out gently. He said, "Sarah, you do know that the Lord expects you to come to Him messy, right? You don't have to come to Him perfectly put together for Him to love you. He loves you because He is good, and His love for you doesn't go up or down based on your performance."

That priest's loving words were not a new concept to me, but I needed the reminder that God's love is not like human love. Our hurts and wounds from the past can leave us guarded, and sometimes (even without knowing it) we can feel as if we have to "keep it all together" and "play the part," constantly playing the game of trying to become worthy to be loved by our Lord. It can be so easy to feel like the woman at the well. "Why is this man talking to me? *If he only knew who I am or what I've done*, then he wouldn't be talking to me."

And yet in His own way, Jesus gently says to her: "I know it all. And I see you. I desire a relationship with you. Please know you are beautiful to me."

It can be easy to think that this person or this job or this commitment or even your motherhood or control of a situation will make you happy or will be the fulfillment you desire. But at any age or stage of your life, all those good things will inevitably come up short. When we try to make idols or gods out of those goods, we put an immense amount of pressure on those things or people, and when they inevitably fail or come up short, we end up disappointed.

This is a hard truth, but one that I have found to be true in my life. I am the firstborn and only girl in my family, a recovering type-A perfectionist people pleaser. I smile as I write this, but that combination has its strengths and weaknesses. And when I was bullied so badly in seventh grade that I had to switch schools, it left me wounded. I spent most of high school doing everything I could to be "enough" and feel loved. And I desperately wanted to be liked, never to feel that same rejection and dismissal I felt in junior high. That life was *exhausting*, and it was definitely a game of "I will be happy *if and when* ..." and it left me with many insecurities, fears, and wounds.

As the pressures of college mounted and relationships fell apart, I fought bitterness and anger; I fought the "I need to get my life together so I can go back to Mass and God." I dodged Him and others. I felt as if I needed to put up walls and façades to keep everyone (even God) at a distance, for at a distance, no one could see me or hurt me. In a way, I was like the woman at the well, avoiding the other women in the morning, trudging to the well alone, with a heavy jar and the weight of a hopeless ache, bordering on despair—just going through the motions.

Maybe you have experienced a reality like this; maybe you've walked that road with a friend or have had a friend who ignored you and hid behind "I'm fine—nothing's wrong." There are many women at the well, all with different stories and backgrounds and wounds. But one thing is sure: we are all on a journey, and we all need water. And there is a Man sitting on the edge of that well with a warm smile, a penetrating gaze, a deep understanding of our plight, and a firm resolution not to give up on us, offering a simple request: "Give me your heavy jar; give me permission to heal your heart, to love you and make you whole. Allow me to walk with you and give you the satisfying water of eternal life."

We can't do this without Him. He is the answer, and He gives the water of eternal life, which is the drink that will make us never thirst again. We can look and look and play the "I'll be happy *if and when* ..." game, but in the end, through the good and the bad, the heartache and the joy, the struggles and the victories, we need Him. And we need each other. We need the other women at the well with us.

When I was slowly letting the Lord back into my life in college and slowly starting the road to healing, I went on a retreat and met some young Catholic women. I had never had close Catholic female friends before. I remember feeling that the Lord was nudging me toward them, and all I could think was, "Oh no, Lord, please, anyone but women. I don't trust women as far as I can throw them." I didn't want to be a pawn in their chess game and didn't want to get in the middle of the gossip or cattiness that sometimes plagues groups of women. I didn't want the comparing, competition, one-upping, and feelings of inadequacies that result from just being in their presence. A lot of those preconceived notions were from my wounded past, but I think many of us have experienced the unintentional (or sometimes quite intentional) daggers from other women at various stages of life.

As something of an antidote, I have always loved the relationship between Mary and Elizabeth, and I love praying with the first chapter of Luke's Gospel. Listen to these words and imagine this scene:

> In those days Mary arose and went with haste into the hill country, to a city of Judah, and she entered the house of Zechariah and greeted Elizabeth. And when Elizabeth heard the greeting of Mary, the babe leaped in her womb; and Elizabeth was filled with the Holy Spirit and she exclaimed with a loud cry, "Blessed are you among women, and blessed is the fruit of your womb! And why is this granted

me, that the mother of my Lord should come to me? For behold, when the voice of your greeting came to my ears, the babe in my womb leaped for joy. And blessed is she who believed that there would be a fulfilment of what was spoken to her from the Lord." (vv. 39-45)

Place yourself in Mary's and Elizabeth's shoes. Mary has had something amazing happen to her; she was probably shocked and a bit confused and, as we might say in this day and age, "feeling all the feels!" And the first thing she does (with *haste*) is run to Elizabeth. What she finds in Elizabeth is kindness, warmth, encouragement, humility, strength, and not one drop of competition or angst or jealousy. Remember, Elizabeth is carrying a child also; it might have been easy for her to have said (with her hands on her hips): "Hmph, what makes you so special, Mary? Why did God the Father choose you to bear the Messiah? Is my baby not good enough? Am I not good enough?"

No. Elizabeth was happy for Mary, was proud of Mary, and was *there for Mary* at a time of great need. They were there for each other. Both Mary and Elizabeth, and their sons and stories, play a huge role in salvation history, and it all began with each of them knowing the love of God in their hearts. They saw everything as a gift from God and placed their trust in Him. Even during tough times and watching a plan unfold that they may not have understood at the time, they gave their fiat and were rooted in these truths and rooted in friendships that always pointed toward Him and toward Heaven.

Like Mary and Elizabeth, like the women in Samaria, we are also women at the well, and we have a choice. We can take our heavy jars to the well every day and worry and gossip and come and go and feel anxious and unsatisfied, or we can go to the well and take our heavy jars and hand them to the Lord. We can hand over the fear, especially the nagging fear of not being enough or doing enough or not being loved. We can fall into the Lord's arms and rest in the truth that He sees us—our wounds and all—and that He loves us. And we can walk arm in arm with our friends and sisters in Christ as we encourage and pray for one another.

And we can emulate one last part of the Samaritan's story: she shared her encounter with Jesus with other Samaritans—and many of them came to believe in Jesus because of her testimony (John 4:39).

When our lives are changed, they become beacons of light for others.

God wants us to
do great things
for Him, and the
greatest thing of all
is our own holiness.

MOTHER ANGELICA

CHAPTER 14

WHO ARE YOU?

Johnnette B. Williams

For thou didst form my inward parts,
thou didst knit me together in my mother's womb.
I praise thee, for thou art fearful and wonderful.
Wonderful are thy works!
Thou knowest me right well;
my frame was not hidden from thee,
when I was being made in secret,
intricately wrought in the depths of the earth.

Thy eyes beheld my unformed substance;
in thy book were written, every one of them,
the days that were formed for me,
when as yet there was none of them.
How precious to me are thy thoughts, O God!"

PSALM 139:13–17

I remember very well the first moment I knew who I was. It was startling, amazing, and downright exhilarating, and I wanted to shout it from the rooftops! Now, just to be clear, I hadn't been suffering from amnesia, nor was I uncertain about my origins. I was in my right mind, and I had been raised by my biological parents.

But it wasn't until that moment that I truly knew *who* I was—the deepest part of my identity—and it was liberating. I wanted to proclaim it to the whole world, and that's what I've been doing for the past forty-plus years of my life.

It all began when I started to practice my Faith again. I was born and raised a Catholic and had attended twelve years of Catholic school before I went off to university. Frankly, however, in my senior year of high school, I became ambivalent about my Faith. I began to question things that I once would never have questioned.

It was a strange time. Everything seemed to be up for grabs. The culture was changing rapidly, and the moral truths that held everything together were being challenged. People my age were pushing boundaries and redefining what was good, true, and beautiful. Catchphrases, heralding an ideology that ditched God and put man at the center of all things, were being drummed into impressionable minds through every form of media. "Turn on, tune in, drop out." "If it feels good, do it." "Let your freak flag fly." "Question authority." Slogans like these illustrate the intoxicating messages that led many young people out of churches and into streets to revolt against the established norms.

Even things in the Catholic Church seemed to be up for grabs. The Second Vatican Council had recently closed, and its beautiful documents were being misrepresented by progressive elites within the Church. The misinterpretations were not without effect. Changes to the sacred liturgy unintentionally ushered in an opportunity for liturgical abuse, adults were questioning Church teaching on issues such as contraception and abortion, and consecrated religious and priests were abandoning their convents and parishes.

The winds of change were felt everywhere, even in the small steel-mill town where I attended Catholic high school. Imperceptibly, I began to breathe in the air of discontent and moral relativism[26] that was permeating the cultural mindset. Although my education was a traditional one, and religious Sisters were my primary educators, it was impossible to ignore the fact that "the times they were a-changin'."[27] For me, all of the changes were jarring—and yet enticing!

When I went off to university, I was ripe for the college scene of the time. My waning interest in the Faith, the mantras of the day, and the seductive ideologies and philosophies presented in classrooms and regurgitated in pubs all stewed together into a brew that became irresistible to me.

Make no mistake about it, however. The blame—and the consequences—are all mine. I could have resisted. But I didn't. I succumbed. How much sin, suffering, and senseless musing I could have avoided had I chosen to drink from the living water of my Catholic Faith rather than from the Kool-Aid of the moment.

Aware of the situation of the day, the Church offered instruction and direction to Her children to guide them through the turbulent waters they were navigating. The very document that had been misused to seemingly align the Church with the spirit of the age, the Decree on the Apostolate of the Laity, reminded the lay faithful of the perilous waters swirling about them. It warned them that new problems and *very* serious errors were circulating "which tend to undermine the foundations of religion, the moral order, and human society itself."[28]

---

[26] A belief that truth, morality, and reality are subjective rather than objective and can be determined by the individual.

[27] Adapted from the name of the Bob Dylan tune "The Times They Are A-Changin'."

[28] Second Vatican Council, Decree on the Apostolate of the Laity *Apostolicam Actuositatem* (November 10, 1965), no. 6.

To avoid the cultural undertow, the Church pointed the faithful to holiness of life and encouraged them to conform their lives to their Faith rather than to the mores of the world.[29] She instructed them to "make progress in holiness in a happy and ready spirit, trying prudently and patiently to overcome difficulties" and reminded them that their success "depends upon ... living [in] union with Christ."[30] Ten years later, I would read these words and see the wisdom and the truth behind them. But not then.

I graduated from university, married, had three children, and was a high school English teacher. Although I no longer participated in the same kind of activities as I had in my college days, certain patterns of behavior and their consequences clung to me. Clinging to me, too, was the sense of interior desolation that had gripped me in those years.

The hype of the sixties and the seventies had fallen short. Rather than experiencing the freedom and fulfillment that the rant of the day promised, I felt trapped, miserable, at odds with myself. And nothing could shake the haunting feeling that I was lost. What had happened to the little girl who once knew loving and friendly discourse with God? Or the young lady who toyed with the idea of religious life? Who was this woman she had become—the one who felt dead inside no matter how she tried to rouse herself to life?

In Romans, St. Paul writes, "the wages of sin is death" (6:23), and such was the case for me. Death had come to my soul as a result of the sinful choices I had made, and the misery of my condition was my just earning. The life I had been living was devoid of God, His presence, and the gift of His divine life. Time and again,

[29] Ibid., no. 13.
[30] Ibid., no. 4.

I had chosen against Him in favor of my own willful action, and little by little, I snuffed out His life within me. My spirit died, and when the spirit dies, as the song from the late sixties proclaims, we "come undone."[31] I was reaping the bitter consequences of my actions, just like our first parents, Adam and Eve.

You recall the story. In Genesis, we read that God *chose* to create man[32] (Gen. 1:26) and that He created him in His image

---

[31] "She's Come Undone," The Guess Who, 1969.

> She's come undone / She didn't know what she was headed for / And when I found what she was headed for / It was too late.

> She's come undone / She found a mountain that was far too high / And when she found out she couldn't fly / It was too late.

> Refrain: It's too late / She's gone too far / She's lost the sun / She's come undone / She wanted truth / But all she got was lies / Came the time to realize / And it was too late.

> She's come undone / She didn't know what she was headed for / And when I found what she was headed for / Mama, it was too late.

> Refrain

> Too many mountains and not enough stairs to climb / Too many churches and not enough truth / Too many people and not enough eyes to see / Too many lives to lead and not enough time.

> Refrain

> She didn't know what she was headed for / And when I found what she was headed for / It was too late.

[32] "Man" is used here in the traditional sense, referring to the totality of humanity, inclusive of the two sexes, male and female.

and likeness (see Gen. 1:27). The human person[33] is a composite of body and soul, and it is by way of the rational soul that man images God. Through the gift of our personhood, God shares aspects of His divine life with us. Like Him, we have rationality (the ability to think and reason), we have self-consciousness (we know we exist), and we have free will (the ability to choose and make decisions, giving us the capacity for self-governance). In all creation, only man has received this bestowal; it separates him from the animals and the rest of the created order. And it is through these God-imaging gifts that we come to know God and have the capacity to act upon that knowledge.

But there is more. "God is love," says Sacred Scripture (1 John 4:16), and in this we most profoundly image God. In fact, love defines the *imago Dei*, the "image of God." Through our personhood, we are capable of receiving the love of God and loving Him and others in return (see 1 John 4:19–21). And it is in this that we find ultimate fulfillment, joy, peace, contentment—and ourselves.

These truths are beautifully conveyed in the Vatican II document *Gaudium et Spes*. It tells us that we are "called as a son to commune with God and share in His happiness"[34] and that one "cannot fully find himself except through a sincere gift of himself."[35] We "find" ourselves and come to know true happiness and joy through knowing God, loving Him, and sharing this love with others.

Before the Fall, Adam lived in this blissful state. His will was one with God's. Complete harmony existed between them, and nothing hindered or marred their relationship. They were in loving union

[33] Angels are also persons created by God, but they are pure spirits.
[34] Second Vatican Council, Pastoral Constitution on the Church in the Modern World *Gaudium et Spes* (December 7, 1965), no. 21.
[35] Ibid., no. 24.

and communed in the "cool of the day" (Gen. 3:8). This intimate harmony with God produced an interior harmony in Adam. Filled with God's love and life, his passions and his bodily appetites (his lower powers) were rightly ordered and subject to his reason and his will (his higher powers). He was one within himself—an integrated whole. This interior harmony or integrity, in turn, flowed to the rest of creation, producing an exterior harmony between Adam and the created order. Remember that Adam had dominion over the things of the earth. Because his higher powers ruled his passions and appetites, Adam had no inordinate desire to abuse the things of the world or to overindulge in them. He was "rightly ordered," and that over which he had dominion functioned accordingly.

In classical spirituality, this is called the "triple harmony": harmony between God and man, between man's soul and his body, and between man and all creation. This was God's plan. And it was perfect, as He is perfect. Man lived in an elevated state, full of grace and full of love, the very essence of the divine life. Man was in harmony with God and at peace within himself. The man and the woman lived in loving union. The animals were docile. The earth produced fruit without the "sweat of the brow." There was no suffering or pain, no sickness or sadness, no disease nor death. This was the heritage that God wanted for you and me. But it was not to be. Through an act of the will, Adam disrupted the triple harmony by sinning against the highest of all three—union with God (Gen. 3:6-7)—and his revolt introduced conflict, disorder, and disintegration into all of creation. And with the sin of Adam, he and everything else came undone.

Instead of integrity, three moral wounds subsequently ruled his heart and mind. St. John describes these as the desires of the flesh (carnal allurements), the enticements of the eye (the allure of worldly things), and the life of "empty show" (the pride in riches) (see 1 John 2:16). Now afflicted by interior disorder and weakened by sin, Adam's intellect was darkened; his passions now ruled his will, and his will fell victim to his lower powers. In shame, he and his wife, Eve, covered themselves and hid from God. When God discovered the pair, Adam blamed his wife for the dreadful action, and she, in turn, blamed the serpent, whose cunning she did not resist.[36] Misery entered the experience of mankind, and all of creation began to groan under its weight (see Rom. 8:22-25).

Through Adam's sin, mankind, including you and me, has inherited Original Sin and concupiscence. The regenerating waters of Baptism take away the stain of Original Sin, but *concupiscence*, the tendency toward sin, remains. With the divine life in us, we can resist. Without it, we will fall. And this was exactly my problem. In living a life devoid of God, drinking in the lies that permeated the culture, and acting out of their faulty premises, I found myself unhappy, unfulfilled, miserable, and disintegrated. This is what accounted for my sense of isolation and being lost. I was adrift, and the plan God wanted for me was thwarted.

But recall: God did not leave His children in this pitiful and desolate state. And He wasn't going to leave me there either. While Adam and Eve were in the midst of their depravity, God promised them a way out. Genesis 3:15, the "protoevangelium" (first gospel), states His plan: "I will put enmity between you and the woman," says God to the evil one, "and between your seed and her seed; he shall bruise your head, and you shall bruise his heel."

---

[36] It is often wondered why Adam is responsible for Original Sin and not Eve. The answer is simply this: Adam was the one charged by God to protect the garden and everything in it, including his wife, Eve (see Gen. 2:15-17). He failed in his duty when he did not protect her from the lure of the devil and did not reject her offer of the fruit.

Although the children of Eve would be born with sin and a tendency to it, they would eventually gain the victory over evil's powers through the Seed of the Woman. The salvific action of her Son, Jesus Christ, the Messiah, would win them the victory,[37] and in time, I would come to know that victory personally.

Thinking I could resolve my inner conflicts with a change of career, I decided to become an insurance agent. I attended the insurance classes with a woman whom I knew casually. I could never have guessed our budding friendship would flower into my reversion to the Faith. But this lovely lady was the very person God would use to bring me back to Him.

She was going through a very difficult time in her life. A smile, however, would eventually break through her tears, and a "confident assurance of things not yet seen" (see Heb. 6:19–20; 1 John 5:14) would light up her face. She was certain God was at work in her sad situation. I was intrigued and began to ask her questions. Her answers to my questions and her invitation to attend a Catholic charismatic prayer meeting set me on a new course of discovery about our Faith and the treasures that are ours by way of it. I became reconciled with God and with His Church in short order.

In those early days of reversion, God in His goodness entrusted to me a Scripture passage that has become the rudder of my spiritual life. In every moment, joyful and sorrowful, this passage has been an anchor that has held me firm. It attended me as I reengaged my Faith, aided me when God called me to apostolic life, sustained me through the ups and downs of serving Him, grounded me when my son was tragically killed, stood by me when

[37] See BibleGateway, s.v. "Genesis 3:15," footnote a, https://www.biblegateway.com/passage/?search=Genesis%203%3A15&version=RSVCE.

my husband died of brain cancer, accompanied me in the happy moments of becoming a grandmother ten times over, and walked down the aisle with me when I married my husband, Jack, after eleven years of widowhood.

Initially, however, this passage identified who I truly was and why I was, and it began a process of healing and restoration that would lead to an ongoing integration of the fractured pieces of my being. See what it says to you:

> Praise be the God and Father of our Lord Jesus Christ, who has bestowed on us in Christ every spiritual blessing in the heavens. God chose us in him before the world began to be holy and blameless in his sight, to be full of love. (Eph. 1:3-4)

As I read this passage for the first time, my blind eyes saw, and my deaf ears heard (see Isa. 35:5). I could never fully express the stunning revelation it spoke to me. Everything in me burst forth with new life! Exuberance flooded my soul! Freedom rang the bell of liberation in my inner being! Peals of gladness sounded in my heart! I was no longer "forsaken" or "desolate" (see Isa. 62:4)! My name was *Chosen Daughter of the Most High God!* This is who I *really* was—my true identity.

The passage continued to inform my understanding. I realized that I was *intentioned* by God, that the thought of me was always in His eternal mind, and that He chose the perfect moment in time to bring me into being. My spirit soared at the very thought of it!

But there was more. God had a great plan in mind for me, and that plan had never changed, regardless of my poor and sinful choices. He was calling me to holiness and blamelessness of life—to sanctity. He was inviting me to be full of His love and to be a conduit of His love in the world! Like the father who waited for the prodigal son, God had been waiting for me, His prodigal daughter. He desired to make me new (see Rev. 21:5), and the process had already begun! And just as the prodigal son's father forgave him, my heavenly Father had forgiven me. In an instant, I understood that "His mercy endures forever" (Dan. 3:67). There was no sin that was unforgivable. If we are truly sorry, repent of our transgressions, and take them to the healing waters of the sacrament of Reconciliation, we will find peace and joy, hope and fortitude, strength and fulfillment. In this way, not the ways of the world, we gain the pearl of great price (see Matt. 13:45-46).

From verse 3, I realized, too, that every second of every day is pregnant with the very blessing we need. Just as I had learned from the *Baltimore Catechism* I read as a child, God was indeed everywhere, and that everywhere included wherever I was. And through His presence, I could receive the grace necessary for every moment if I but chose to receive it and walk in it. In time, I would experience the truth of this verse in the midst of devastating sorrow and grief. Indeed, this passage held the answer to everything I had been searching for.

Ephesians 1:3-4 is as true for you as it is for me. Recall that St. Paul tells the Romans that God doesn't play favorites (Rom. 2:11). What He did for me, He will do for you. You are the beloved daughter of the Most High God. From all eternity, He chose you to have life in Him. He wants you to know Him, to love Him, and to serve Him in this life and to spend all eternity with Him in Heaven. We serve Him by living out our purpose—to cooperate with grace and to progress in holiness and blamelessness of life. In doing so, we attain that which ultimately yields happiness, joy, peace, and true fulfillment. This is what union with God is all about. This is the substance of the spiritual life—a continual growth in intimacy with the One Who made us.

When my husband Anthony died, my girls and I reminisced about the list of "maxims" he had used to instruct and guide them and their brother. We called them *Dadisms*. Strung together, they form a spiritual path that helps us make progress toward union with God. I first recounted them in a booklet I composed to give to those who had come to his viewing. I share them with you here with the hope they will aid you in your walk of faith or provide a starting point to begin that walk. Look at them as a spiritual life guide.

Keep Jesus in front of you.

We cannot arrive at a destination if we don't know where we are going. If our destination is "life on high in Christ Jesus" (see Phil. 3:14), then we must keep Jesus in front of us. To what extent do our thoughts, words, deeds, and motivations conform to Christ? What practical steps do we take on a daily basis to make certain we are making progress? In difficult moments, trying circumstances, reversals, and sorrows, do we turn away from God, or do we turn toward Him? When we fall into sin (serious or otherwise), do we *give up*, or do we *get up* and go to the sacrament of Reconciliation to be made whole once again?

Secure the perimeter.

"Secure the perimeter" is a military term. It refers to the establishment and maintenance of protective measures along the borders of a military installation to safeguard it from enemy infiltration or attack. With the cooperation of grace, we need to guard the perimeter of our souls. We fortify and strengthen our opposition to the enemy through daily prayer; the Holy Sacrifice of the Mass; adoration of the Blessed Sacrament; the sacraments of the Church; the intercession of the saints, especially of the Blessed Mother; sacramentals, such as holy water, blessed salt, and other blessed objects, especially the Scapular and the Miraculous Medal;

devotional practices, primarily the Rosary, our weapon for spiritual warfare,[38] the Chaplet of Divine Mercy, novenas, and litanies. Also consider Consecration to Jesus through Mary using the consecration of St. Louis de Montfort, a spiritual way of life in itself. There is much more to be said about securing the perimeter of our soul, but this is a good beginning. Which of these ways appeal to you? Which of them are already part of your daily practice? Can you add one or two more?

Stay the course.
This maxim seemed to be a favorite of Anthony's for the children and for me. Time and again when I would be facing difficulties in the apostolate or in my personal life, he would tell me, "Johnnette, stay the course." Likewise, he would encourage our three children to stand firm in tough situations. Challenges and struggles, sorrow and suffering are part of this fallen world. What we do in the midst of them makes all the difference. Do we give up and give in? Or do we persevere and move forward in the knowledge that Christ is with us *in those difficulties?*

When trials, big or small, come, I like to picture them as a portion of our Lord's Cross being entrusted to me by God the Father. Doing so not only strengthens me to accept and embrace a trial but also to find joy in it. Our salvation lies in the Cross of Christ, and union with His Cross leads to eternal life (see Matt. 16:24-26). Are you facing a trial right now? Is it possible that this Cross is a holy entrustment—a means to draw closer to Christ?

---

[38] See the book I coauthored with Thomas K. Sullivan, *The Rosary: Your Weapon for Spiritual Warfare*, available through EWTN's Religious Catalogue (ewtnrc.com) or Women of Grace® (womenofgrace.com).

Can you find the joy that is hidden in it?[39] If not, ask our Blessed Lady to help you find it. She will, I assure you.

Finish strong.

Life on earth is a warfare. Our fight is not against flesh and blood but against principalities and powers that rule this present darkness (see Eph. 6:12). We must submit everything to the spiritual guidance and wisdom offered by Holy Mother Church through Her teachings and through Sacred Scripture. Many people today say that the Church has to get with the times. They need to invert their thinking. To make progress in the here and now and for all eternity, the times have to get with the Church!

Pope St. Paul VI made the statement that modern man listens more to witnesses than to teachers. And if he listens to teachers at all, it is because they are witnesses. We are called to be the face of God at this moment. We can reflect Him only to the extent that we part with the ways of the world and its ideologies and live the truth given to us through Sacred Scripture and the teachings of Holy Mother Church. To the extent we accomplish this, we find peace and joy, fulfillment and love. And to the extent we can bring *that* to others, the world will become more Godlike. Isn't this the example of St. John Paul II, St. Teresa of Calcutta, Mother Angelica, and all the other holy men and women of our day and prior times? Remember: this life is a pilgrimage. Our ultimate destination is eternal life. Let us seek to acquire it through and in all of life's circumstances and help others to do the same.

Thus will we all *finish strong!*

---

[39] I have learned time and again that every joy has a cross and every cross has a joy.

The battle they
fought was not one
of swords — swords
that make one
bleed and die; no, it
was a more deadly
battle — a battle of
intellects, of wills, of
ideas and loyalties.

MOTHER ANGELICA

CHAPTER 15

BE AWARE OF YOUR BATTLE

Crystalina Evert

We all have a common enemy—the devil. The *Catechism of the Catholic Church* affirms that Satan exists and is a fallen angel who is envious of us and is a "murderer from the beginning" (see CCC 391, 394). Simply denying this truth does not turn him into an imaginary figure. John 8:44 gives us a clear description of the devil: he is the great deceiver and "the father of lies." 1 Peter 5:8 warns us: "Be sober, be watchful. Your adversary the devil prowls around like a roaring lion, seeking some one to devour." Knowing this, we can understand why demons hide so well and why it is therefore so easy for us to fall into the trap of believing they do not exist.

My spiritual director posed this question to me one day: "Crystalina, which is worse, sin or the devil?" How would you answer that? You see, Satan has power only when we consent to sin. The evil one will always tempt us, but he cannot force us to sin against our will. If our consent is needed for us to sin, and sin directly impacts the state of our souls, we can conclude that sin is much worse.

Ven. Fulton Sheen said: "Before the sin, Satan assures us that it is of no consequence. After the sin, he persuades us that it is unforgivable." When we have wounds, the devil uses them against us. I'm referring to deep-seated wounds and unconfessed sins. When we continue to live in a state of mortal sin, we develop certain habits and vices that eventually erode our souls and even cloud our thinking. In essence, we cooperate with the enemy and become desensitized to sin and the gravity of it. Remaining in this serious state will weaken our will and allow the devil to play on our wounds and insecurities.

On our path to healing, it is essential to break down the obstacles in our spiritual lives. However, confronting those hard truths sometimes means facing the demons that work in our lives and overcoming the vices we struggle with most. We must identify those weaknesses and how they work against us. To give you an example, I used to believe all the lies the evil one was whispering to me. I would internalize the voices of false accusations and self-condemnation. As a result, I carried a tremendous amount of shame and self-loathing. My daily "self-talk" was vicious. I lived as I viewed myself and saw the world around me through a distorted lens. I was completely unaware of the spiritual attack I was under.

When I was ready to undergo an intense healing process, my first step was an honest Confession. At first, I struggled to enter the confessional and was afraid of what my confessor might think of me. It was a humbling experience, but I knew I needed to do it. St. John Chrysostom says, "The Church is a hospital, and not a courtroom, for souls. She does not condemn on behalf of sins but grants remission of sins." Fr. Gabriele Amorth, who was the chief exorcist of the Diocese of Rome, said, "Confession is more effective than an exorcism."[40] Confession keeps the pipeline to God open so we can receive His graces and hear Him. It is extremely powerful and can break strongholds in your life. However, it's not a

---

[40] See Fr. Gabriele Amorth, *An Exorcist Explains the Demonic: The Antics of Satan and His Army of Fallen Angels*, ed. Stefano Stimamiglio, trans. Charlotte J. Fasi (Manchester, NH: Sophia Institute Press, 2016), 87.

one-time occurrence. Keeping ourselves right with God should be part of our monthly routine. I do my best to go every two weeks, and I take my children even if they grumble about it.

It can be challenging to navigate through our faith walks and spiritual battles. Sometimes we need a guide. A regular confessor will help keep you accountable and find patterns in the sins and vices you struggle with most. So pray to find a good priest who can be your spiritual director. It's a sad fact that many people hold themselves back from receiving the sacraments because of clergy who are bad examples. Do not let this keep you from the healing grace that awaits you in the sacraments they administer. There are so many good priests. I am grateful to God for placing in my life holy and courageous priests who have taught me, prayed for me, and spiritually strengthened me for my spiritual battles. Our Catholic Church has immense healing power, and her arms are wide open. The power and anointing that God gives His priests are mighty. Only a priest can consecrate bread and wine to transform them into the Body and Blood of our beloved Jesus. It is a heavenly gift and grace that cannot be matched on earth.

Our Blessed Mother is a powerful aid in our spiritual battles. We often see her portrayed crushing the head of the serpent. The other saint we see depicted as crushing the head of Satan is Michael the Archangel, the commander of God's heavenly army. Our Mother is Queen of Angels. If we ask for the angels' assistance in this spiritual battle, they will not hesitate to come to our aid.

The struggle between good and evil is intensifying. If we are grounded in our Faith and stay close to the sacraments, we will be protected in this battle. Mother Angelica said, "There are two things I want you to do, keep close to Our Lord in the Holy Eucharist and stay close to His Mother. With those two loves, you will always have the light to see what is right and wrong."

The evil one cannot follow you into the light; he can't stand it and will flee. So let the light of God banish the darkness, and arm yourself with the weapons of light.

> Finally, be strong in the Lord and in the strength of his might. Put on the whole armor of God, that you may be able to stand against the wiles of the devil. For we are not contending against flesh and blood, but against the principalities, against the powers, against the world rulers of this present darkness, against the spiritual hosts of wickedness in the heavenly places. Therefore take the whole armor of God, that you may be able to withstand in the evil day, and having done all, to stand. Stand therefore, having girded your loins with truth, and having put on the breastplate of righteousness, and having shod your feet with the equipment of the gospel of peace; above all taking the shield of faith, with which you can quench all the flaming darts of the evil one. And take the helmet of salvation, and the sword of the Spirit, which is the word of God. Pray at all times in the Spirit, with all prayer and supplication. To that end keep alert with all perseverance, making supplication for all the saints. (Eph. 6:10–18)

Our battle against the evil one is a daily struggle. Everyone's fight looks different, but the enemy is the same. What is most important is to be obedient to God's will and proactive in the fight. If we do not use the spiritual weapons God has given us, we will be easy targets. We must therefore learn what they are and how to use them.

Here is an excellent breakdown of the many spiritual weapons at our disposal. It is taken from Kathleen Beckman's *Family Guide to Spiritual Warfare*.

To be effective spiritual warriors capable of wielding defensive and offensive weapons, we must lead an intentional, ordered spiritual life every day. Consider the ideas below.

1. *Sacramental life.* Receive the sacraments with great regularity. If daily Mass is offered, strive to attend.
2. *Scripture.* Read the Bible daily (even for a brief time); reflect on the four Gospels; pray the Psalms; consider Lectio Divina.
3. *Liturgical life.* If possible, pray the Liturgy of the Hours. If you can't pray the full Divine Office, consider using the shorter edition printed in *Magnificat's* monthly booklet. Celebrate the liturgical seasons.
4. *Adoration.* Visit the Blessed Sacrament as frequently as possible; it is very efficacious for healing and holiness.
5. *Virtue.* Strive for growth in the virtues; keep the Ten Commandments and the Beatitudes; prioritize faith and family.
6. *Catholic sacramentals.* Keep sacramentals in your home and on your person. Use holy water, blessed salt, scapulars, a St. Benedict crucifix, and Miraculous Medals.
7. *Daily prayer.* Pray especially for the Lord to heal any area that may have an entryway for evil spirits. For example, if addiction to pornography is your predominant sin, pray specifically for purity and chastity.
8. *Consecration to Jesus through the Virgin Mary, St. Joseph, and St. Michael.* Practice lively devotion to the Holy Family.
9. *Prudence.* Avoid the places and associations that were doorways to any demonic bondage.
10. *Home oratory.* Create an area of the home reserved for prayer, complete with holy articles, and consider it holy ground for prayer only.

11. *The father's blessing.* Fathers, bless your families. Pray for each family member to receive the Eternal Father's blessing.

12. *Home consecration to the Sacred Heart.* Exorcists highly recommend this consecration as protection for the home and family.

13. *Devotion to Our Lady of Sorrows.* For protection, some exorcists recommend praying the Rosary of the Seven Sorrows, also known as the Seven Dolors Rosary.

14. *Holy environment.* In your line of sight, place objects such as icons, crucifixes, and pictures of saints so that your heart is frequently lifted to God.

15. *Sacred music.* Some exorcists recommend playing sacred music such as Gregorian chant in the background to help sanctify the home atmosphere.

16. *Auxilium Christianorum prayers (www.auxiliumchristiano- rum.org).* These include prayers to be said every day and others to be recited on specific days of the week.

17. *Fasting.* Incorporate some form of fasting into your spiritual life to cultivate a spirit of poverty and sacrifice.[41]

The Virgin Mary's Role in Spiritual Combat

The Virgin Mary helps liberate us from evil spirits in the following ways:

1. Mary is the vessel—the Mediatrix—of God's grace. God anointed her for spiritual warfare as the most powerful

---

[41] Kathleen Beckman, *A Family Guide to Spiritual Warfare: Strategies for Deliverance and Healing* (Manchester, NH: Sophia Institute Press, 2020), 208–209.

threat to Satan because of her extraordinary union with Jesus.

2. Because God chose the Virgin Mary to be the New Eve against demons, the name of Mary has a similar impact to the name of Jesus. This is seen during exorcisms.

3. Mary's holy maternal presence is extraordinarily painful to demons. They know the efficacy of Marian intervention. The Incarnation—the undoing of the devil—was fulfilled in Mary.

4. Mary's virtues and union with the Holy Spirit make her a fierce destroyer of diabolical plots and tactics. Her life-giving love and defense of God's family are infuriating to prideful demons.[42]

One of the Church's most common prayers for protection is the prayer to St. Michael the Archangel:

St. Michael the Archangel, defend us in battle. Be our defense against the wickedness and snares of the devil. May God rebuke him, we humbly pray; and do thou, O Prince of the heavenly host, by the power of God, thrust into hell Satan and all the evil spirits who prowl about the world seeking the ruin of souls. Amen.

---

[42] Ibid., 238.

The essence of
evangelization is to
tell everybody that
Jesus loves you!

MOTHER ANGELICA

CHAPTER 16

PEOPLE IN PERSONAL PRISONS

Mother Angelica

I f you understood some simple truths, you could overcome anything. You could overcome any fault, any sin, any weakness.
Why? Because we were known to God before the foundation
of the world—before He created a star, before He created an atom,
He knew me; He knew you! Isn't that wonderful? Why don't you
try to think of that when you wake up in the morning instead of
saying, "Oh God, another day?" It's a wonderful day!

Is it wonderful? No, it may be miserable. Life stinks sometimes.
It does, and there's nothing you can do about it. You're in a miserable situation. It's going to be there today; it's going to be there
tomorrow until something happens, something changes. But why
be unhappy about it?

You say, "Oh, Mother, you never suffer." Don't you say that. If
you've never lived in a rat-infested apartment—and I don't mean
these little mice you scream about; I mean sewer rats—then life
hasn't been that hard on you.

But see, I wish I would have known when I was a kid that
the Lord loved me. I didn't know the Lord until I was eighteen.
That's a long time to live as a Catholic and not know Jesus, don't
you think? That's the way it was, and I didn't know Him. I knew
there was a God, and I believed, and I could recite the *Catechism*
questions and answers, but I didn't understand them. And nobody
told me that Jesus loved me! I knew He loved everybody, but it's
different when you know He loves *you*! I didn't know that. I didn't

know that till He healed me. Then I knew a lot. I knew He loved me; I knew He healed me and somehow chose me, but I didn't know why, and I didn't know if He really did.

I think most people are like that. They live their entire lives and think they're only a grain of sand on the seashore. But you're special! And that's not positive thinking. It's a fact. There's a difference. And Jesus talks about how you fed Him when He was hungry, gave Him drink when He was thirsty, welcomed Him and clothed Him when He was a stranger and naked, visited Him when He was sick, went to see Him when He was in prison (see Matt. 25:31–46). You say, "Well, I've never been to prison in my life." Oh, maybe the man or woman sitting next to you is in prison. Some of you are in prison. Oh, you're out, meaning you're "free." But are you free? Do you know God? Are you sorry for your sins? If not, then you're not free.

I went to a big federal prison and gave a talk to the prisoners. And one thing I remember saying to them is this: "I know you're in prison, but in here, you don't have to be." We talked about the Lord, and I told them there are more people in prison outside those walls than there were inside. Think about it.

Well, after it was over, I said to them, "I'm going to say a prayer for you, okay?" And they all nodded their heads, and I opened my eyes, and they had lined up next to me. And this young man said to me, "Would you pray just for me?" I said, "Oh, yes!" And so I prayed over him. And this man had to be almost seven feet tall. I mean, I never saw somebody so tall in my life, and he leaned over so I could touch his head. And I prayed for him as if he were just a child. And I thought, "How awesome, that these men in prison suddenly looked so free, as if they finally found out the one truth necessary." I never saw such a gentle group of men.

A lot of people are in error, a lot of people are in prison, because they have never known they are loved by God. What a terrible thing that perhaps they were not taught simple things, basics. This world is so brainy—too brainy. We're like robots or something. We've just got too much in our heads. How much is in our hearts?

When I visited that prison, I felt sure that there were more people in prison outside the prison than there were inside. I remember going through the double gate and all the police up on a big wall and lights going off and on. I remember the prisoner who brought me in. I looked at him and said, "Did you know Jesus loves you so much?" He looked so surprised—like, "Who would love me?" And when he opened the door and brought me back out, we went through the yard, we went through the gates, and he looked at me and sighed, and he said, "Thank you. I think it'll be better here now."

All the people in prison outside—maybe if you just told them that? When was the last time you said to anybody, "Did you know Jesus loves you?" Well, I bet you don't because you're afraid of being a fanatic. Hey, be one. It's okay. A lot of people say, "You're a fanatic, Mother." I don't care. That's my duty. It's your duty too. You'll never know, my friend, what awesome things are wrought in other people's souls by telling them they are loved by God so very much. And I think that's what our dear Lord meant. It wasn't just going into a prison—because I'm convinced that today young people are in prison. They can't stop what they're doing. They can't stop the drugs; they can't stop the lust; they can't stop the alcohol. They can't stop. It's like a madness. That's a prison, isn't it?

When you hate somebody and you won't forgive, isn't that a prison? You wake up with it in the morning, go to bed with it at night—oh, are you in prison!

Do you know that a lot of children don't ever visit their parents? I'll never forget the time I went to a convalescent home and the nurse said, "This poor lady's always crying. We don't know how to help her."

I went in there. I said, "Hey, God loves you! What's wrong?"

She said, "I have eleven children."

I said, "Oh, God bless you."

And she looked at me, and she said, "Did He?"

I said, "I think so."

She said, "I haven't seen one of them in four years."

Isn't that a prison—to know you raised eleven kids, and you clothed them, and you cooked for them, and you did everything you could for them—and in four years, not one came to visit? She didn't look like a mean old lady to me.

And if you tell me that you deliberately don't visit your mother in a convalescent home, you're worse than in prison. Somewhere along the line, that's Hell. I think it is because there has to be a kind of selfishness and greed that doesn't care about your mother or your father or anybody, only what you can get and get more of.

And see, our Lord is saying something different. "You didn't visit me." You say, "Oh, that's only my mother." No! It's God, the One Who gave you birth, the One Who raised you, brought you into the world, cried when you cried, loved you when you were sick, and forgave you when you were wrong. That's the Lord.

You'll want to watch it because He'll look at you one day and say, "I was sick, and you didn't visit me." That's what it means. "I was naked, and you didn't clothe me." What does that mean—to go around buying clothes for everybody? No.

Aren't some of you naked of truth? How many of you even know God? How many Catholics have been told, "That's not the Eucharist. That's just a symbol"? When that happens, somebody strips you totally naked of truth. The worst kind of nakedness is not to be told the truth! When somebody doesn't tell you the truth about God, he strips you naked. What do you have? You don't have the truth! Well, what happens when you don't have the truth? You live by an error. You live by a lie. Oh boy, that's a nakedness you don't want to have, my friends. You could have beautiful clothes on and be stripped of grace.

But my good friend the Curé of Ars—I'm not old enough to really have been his friend, but he belongs to the Church Triumphant, so he's my friend. When a great actress, clothed with the most expensive clothing you could buy in those days, came in a carriage, very fancy, the whole city of Ars was out to see that celebrity. The curé went to meet her. She got out of the carriage with great dignity and pomp. The curé said, "Madam, excuse me, but the stench of your soul makes me vomit."

The Lord isn't talking about clothes. He's talking about sanctifying grace.

Somebody told you the Eucharist is only a symbol. Somebody told you our Lord is only there for Mass. No! If you believe that, you're naked because you don't have the divine garment on.

And then our Lord says, "I was thirsty; you gave me no drink." What is that, now? He's talking about a glass of water? No. This is judgment, my friends. We're not talking about pizza and pasta. *Thirsty.*

Has anybody ever asked you a question about God—thirsty for God—knowing in their heart there has to be something more than the vacuum they're living in? And what do you say? "Oh, I wouldn't pay attention to that. It's not important." That person was thirsting for God, and you turned away.

This is a very important passage of St. Matthew. We're just so sure it means food and drink and clothes; it doesn't have anything to do with that. Our dear Lord never wasted time on that. He said, "Consider the lilies, how they grow; they neither toil nor spin; yet I tell you, even Solomon in all his glory was not arrayed like one of these" (Luke 12:27).

"I was a stranger, and you did not welcome me." Who are strangers today? Well, everybody can be a stranger if you're an old fuddy duddy, if you don't like people, don't like anything—a kind of Scrooge in the middle of summer, one of these kinds of people never happy about anything, never satisfied about anything, and there's always something wrong somewhere. If they bought a brand-new car, they'd find a scratch on it under the hood. You can't win! But what is our Lord saying here? He's saying, "Have you talked to me about the other world?"

People come to see you maybe after supper, and they stay, and they stay, and they stay. And you yawn, and they stay, and you look at your watch, and they stay. I mean, it looks like a midnight thing. Not to worry! I'll tell you how to get rid of them. Talk about Heaven, death, Purgatory. "Oh, I've got to go! It's getting so late!" It may be later than you think, my friend. So next time that happens at your house, try it! You'll be surprised. You could be having a party, and they'll all go, every single one. And maybe that's what God wants you to do.

I called a disc jockey friend of mine. I said, "How much would it cost me to request a silent record?"

He said, "What?"

I said, "A silent record."

He said, "What's that mean?"

I said, "You just play nothing for three minutes."

He said, "Are you crazy? I'll lose my audience."

I said, "Well, that says something, doesn't it? We can't stand the pressure of being alone with God for three minutes."

I would have paid him, but he didn't want to take a chance. Chicken!

Love our Lord. If you love someone, that someone is on your mind often, depending on the kind of love you have for that person.

The whole essence of becoming holy is to do God's will. To love is to do. You've got the Commandments, the beauty of the Church, the Eucharist, our Lady, all the unbelievable doctrines we have and dogmas. Then you keep those because when you keep them, then God is always in your heart.

Our Lord says, "If you keep my commandments, the Father and I will come." And do what? "Make our home in you" (see John 14:23). Oh, wow! So if your heart is free, and God lives in you, then you're going to do His will readily. Why? Because you want to please Him, see? I don't think it's hard to be holy. I think it's hard to be unholy. You never feel guilty if you're doing God's will. If you're not doing God's will, you feel guilty. Running around with all that guilt on your heart—that's not easy! I think it's hard to be a sinner.

But to love God is to love Him. This doesn't have to do with feelings. I want to be like Him—that's what it means. And I want to be like Him because He loves me. And if I want to love Him, I want to act as He would act. Do we do this all the time? No, but we can say, "I'm sorry, Lord, I didn't come up to Your expectations, but I'm going to try harder tomorrow." It's easier to be holy. Maybe the initial effort is hard, but you can get in the habit of being holy and just say, "Jesus, I love You. I want to be like You today." And when you're not, say, "I'm sorry. I'm going to try harder." Simple. It frees our minds and frees our hearts. Why? Because you know a truth—the Father, the Son, and the Holy Spirit live in you. That's holiness.

Confession

Let's pretend I have a barrel, one of these old-fashioned barrels, and I want to fill it with water, but I've only got a tablespoon. It's going to take me a long time to fill it, one tablespoon at a time. So venial sins can pile up, but what can happen? My will becomes weaker and weaker and weaker, one tablespoon at a time. The first thing you know, I don't have any sense anymore, and so I can get into bigger sins because I've lost that sense of sin. And not only that, but I'm displeasing the Lord and not coming up to His expectations.

He wants every one of us to live in Him as the Trinity lives in each other. "As the Father loves me, I love you," He said (see John 15:9). Wow! He told St. Catherine of Siena, "Since you cannot love Me with an infinite love, I take your love, the love you give to your neighbor, as done to Me." Well, I love you; I love Jesus. See, isn't that wonderful? So you go and find a holy priest who can not only help you with your fault or your venial sin but can help you overcome and help you get a confidence and trust in God that He will help you.

When he says, "I absolve you from all your sins," those are the most beautiful words you could ever hear.

Do you know what I would do if I were afraid of going to Confession? I would offer that up as my penance. You might as well make something good out of it. What I would do is to say, "Jesus, I offer You this fear. I offer it to You in reparation for all my sins, all the fears of everybody, and unite it with the fear You had in the Agony in the Garden." Once you take something like that and give it to Jesus and unite it with His fear in the Agony in the Garden, it does something for you. You go in to Confession filled with Jesus.

It's easy for me to say, "Don't be afraid." I've never been afraid of Confession. I have a lot of other fears, but I don't have that one. I can understand it because a lot of people have it. Sometimes they don't overcome it; they don't go to Confession. But Confession is important. Sometimes you may have a big intention in your heart; for example, you want something for your husband, your children, your friends, your family. Well, if you fear going to Confession, offer that fear as a sacrifice. Just say, "Lord, I offer this sacrifice to You for this intention." Don't let anything go to waste. Don't let your fears go to waste. Don't let your pain go to waste. Give Jesus the joy of saying, "Look, she went to Confession even though she was scared to death." That shows real love for the Lord.

God's Will

I don't think we should question God at all, because it's like putting the ocean in a capsule. You can't. And that's the difference with love. If you love someone, as we should love God, sometimes we can wonder but never question. We had a lot of problems here at the beginning of this network—an awful lot of problems. And I was sick; I had all kinds of pain and everything else. And we were in debt. The network was seemingly going down the tube. It was just everything wrong. And I was angry. I didn't know anything about this business, didn't want to know anything about it, and there I was.

And I went to the chapel—we have our dear Lord exposed all the time. And I said, "Lord, we're going down, and I told You I don't know anything about this stuff! And everything's happening. Why me?" And then I heard a very gentle voice, and He said with a sigh, "Yes, and why me?"

Well, I never asked that question again. He has a right to do what He wills with all of us, any of us, and we should have the love and knowledge to know that nothing happens to us that is not for our good if we love Him. He's our Father; He's our Savior; He's our Lord; He came and lived among us and was murdered by us and rose again. He gave us an unbelievable Church. He gave us Himself in the Eucharist. After all of that, why do we doubt? Why? We shouldn't spend any time asking *why* of God. Do it, whatever it is. And when you get to Heaven, you'll know, but who cares after that?

God's Will and Faith

When you pray, pray with faith—not presumption but faith, ready for a yes or no, knowing that God is able and that He is the Lord God.

"What is Your will, Lord? Tell me. I'll be content."

Now, that should happen every time or any time you're in front of the Holy Eucharist. He has never left us. He's still with us; He's still here. We have the same Jesus. I don't know why it's so hard to accept that, and He calls us all, so go to Jesus.

In the Cleveland monastery where I started, they had a six-foot statue of St. Joseph. In gold letters, it said "*Ite ad Joseph,*" "Go to Joseph." But we ought to say, "Go to the Blessed Sacrament; go to Jesus."

Sometimes for your sake, God has to say no. I can think of a lot of prayers I'm so glad God said no to. Aren't you glad you didn't marry the man you almost married? Aren't you glad you didn't marry the woman you almost married? Many times you are, and in all of your problems and difficulties, who brought you through? Jesus.

Suffering

Now, I'm going to talk to you a little bit about what St. Paul says about suffering. We don't think like this at all, but a wise person thinks like this. Suffering and understanding of suffering and the understanding of wisdom go together. Okay, what does St. Paul say about suffering? He says, "By faith we are judged righteous and at peace with God." (Rom. 5:1).[43]

When I have a fear, I'm not at peace with God, am I?

So you can see where fear and lack of trust sometimes go together, right? Well, we're going to see how fear and wisdom can go together to overcome this fear we have. We have fears of everything. Some people have fear of swallowing pills. My mother was that way. I had to grind everything up, and I disguised it in everything. I tried jelly one time. She wouldn't swallow a pill, and I ground it up, and I put it in jelly.

But now St. Paul talks about sufferings. These are real sufferings—nothing you can go to a doctor about. Sometimes you don't want to tell your neighbors, for fear they'll think you're a kind of wacko or something. Some people can't go up twelve inches; they're afraid. Some people are afraid to go outside. We need to get rid of all these fears. Now, St. Paul says, "Sufferings bring patience" (Rom. 5:3). Does your suffering bring patience? "Patience brings perseverance" (Rom. 5:4). A lot of people are afraid of goofing off at the last minute. "Perseverance brings hope" (Rom. 5:4). The person who hopes doesn't have too much trouble with fear. There is a kind of correlation between suffering, patience, perseverance, and now hope. We can have a lot of problems; we can have all kinds of frustrations. But if I have hope, I won't fear.

Wisdom and Suffering

They say as you get older, you get wise. Is that true? Nah, it isn't always true. Old age by itself doesn't bring wisdom. Experience

[43] Scripture quotations in this chapter are taken from the Jerusalem Bible, © 1966 by Darton Longman and Todd Ltd. and Doubleday and Company Ltd.

does sometimes, but there are all kinds of wisdom. There's natural wisdom, but natural wisdom must be mixed with prudence. Sometimes, you get advice from somebody, and you say, "That's so wise." You can tell that there's enough experience there, that they've gone through it, they've felt it, and they see something in a situation that you don't see at all; but there's always that virtue of prudence. Prudence is like a balance. It keeps me from going down or up. It's like that balance that you have in the spiritual life.

Now, Solomon prayed for wisdom, didn't he? What was the wisdom Solomon prayed for? Well, he prayed to govern his people, he prayed that he might make right decisions, he prayed that he would understand the ways of God, and he wrote beautifully about wisdom. Then there is the wisdom that comes from the Holy Spirit. That wisdom is a supernatural gift from God that makes me very much aware of the presence of God in my daily life to the point where God is uppermost in my mind and the most important One in my life. That's the gift of wisdom.

You can say, "I'm afraid of heights. I'm afraid of being hurt again. I'm afraid at my job." We all have fear. Sometimes, if you talk it over, you feel better about it. We're all family here. We're going to pray and ask the Lord to take away that fear because it was always a question in the Lord's mind: "Why do you fear?"—as if He didn't quite understand. Most fear comes from a lack of trust: "I don't trust these people. I don't trust the world. I don't trust politicians." Well, it's kind of hard to do that these days, isn't it?

Complaining and Suffering

Well, we need more faith. I know what pain is; I have it all the time. And I know your poor human nature gets overly tired sometimes, and you get tired of pain. But that's where the Rosary comes in, and that's where the Sorrowful Mysteries come in, if you say them and look at Jesus. Today, we don't believe in crucifixes anymore, but I carry mine, and all during Mass I'm able to hold on to Him. We need that extra grace. We need to know how precious suffering is.

I feel sorry for myself once in a while, but we can't allow that to last too long. You can't help feeling sorry for yourself. You can't help hurting. You can't help the duration. But you can say, "Jesus, You suffered so much for me." He didn't have to. He was very happy with His Father in Heaven. He didn't have to suffer, and He suffered so much! Oh, we'll never know in this life.

This is your wonderful opportunity. The Father looks down on you with special love because as you suffer, He sees His Son in you. He does! And if you're offering it up, as you say, what a wonderful thing! You can change the world.

Pray for priests, religious, our Holy Father, all the faithful, the sick, the dying. You have so much to pray for. And when you get to Heaven, you'll see all of these souls coming toward you. You'll say, "Who are you?" And they'll say, "Your prayers gave us the grace. The Lord heard your prayers and gave us extra grace to say we were sorry for all our sins."

How do you like that? Our God is a wonderful God. He's compassionate and merciful and loving. And we do feel very bad over what goes on in the Church, and the world too—how deceived we are with abortion and all that. But we can never forget the Lord has all of us in His hands. He will not forsake us.

The Church and the world will one day rise again with great hope and love and holiness. We won't even believe what it's going to be like. Have courage, then, and hope. The Lord is greater than the world and Satan and all his demons and greater than all the leaders of this world. And one day, He will come and shepherd us Himself, and we will see Him as He is.

Lord Jesus, we all have fears for one reason or another, and there are so many out there who have all kinds of fears — fears that keep them from You, fears that keep them from loving, fears that keep them from being what they should be. Lord, extend Your hand and take away their fear. Give them that kind of trust in Your love, in Your providence, in Your goodness — most of all, in Your love for them personally, as if no one else existed. Take away the guilt of their past sins. Take away their fear of tomorrow. Take away every fear in their lives. I ask this in Your Most Holy Name and through the intercession of Mary our Holy Mother.

God bless you. Don't be afraid.
Remember only one thing: God loves you, and so do I!

LETTER TO WOMEN

Crystalina Evert

Why do you always seek man's approval? You're always wondering: "Do I look pretty enough? Do I sound smart enough?" With a shadow of insecurity hovering above you, you're always trying to keep others interested. Meanwhile, you give yourself away while ignoring your gut. Don't be controlled by the amount of attention and approval you receive, and stop being ashamed of yourself. Your worth can't come from the people you're with, what you wear, or what others think of you.

Are you scared to admit your self-worth? Do you keep your true beauty, gifts, and talents so locked away and hidden from the world that you can't truly see how amazing you are? Are you afraid of shining so brightly that the light will scare others away? Do not shy from who you are because you fear abandonment or the negative opinions of others. You take scraps from the world, but you have everything you need, deep within you. Everyone's light is different, and some are brighter than others. But do not be scared of your own light, for it was put in you so that others who are blinded by their own darkness could see your light.

Why are you scared and sad? Why do you belittle yourself and dim your light? Your light was made to shine; that is its purpose. Your self-worth is within you and has been given to you for a purpose. Your beauty—God's beauty—was given for a great reason as well. The darkness has tried to extinguish this beauty within, but it cannot. It will not be put out.

At times, you allow your insecurities to overpower you, and your thoughts run wild. But with Jesus' love, you can resist any vice, wickedness, or evil weapon that comes against you. It's time to rise up, unafraid of who you are. Embrace who you are. "Do not lower yourself or hide," God says, "because the power of my love and grace will always be there to catch you and show you the way. I will catch you, but will you let me?"

Deep down, you know who you are and what you are supposed to do. Stop lowering yourself to the world and start rising to Heaven. Even though it might seem far away, it truly is all around you. Heaven is watching, praying, and cheering you on. You have a whole army of angels and saints wanting you to succeed in your battle. But the biggest battle of all will be with yourself. Know who you are and what you are not. You are a beloved daughter of Jesus, He Who is God.

INSPIRATION FROM SCRIPTURE

*If God gives you the burden, God
will give you the strength.*

ST. JOSEMARÍA ESCRIVÁ, *FORGE* 325

Get inspired by the word of God:

Worry   1 Peter 5:7   Isaiah 26:3

                John 14:1   Proverbs 3:24

                John 14:27

Loneliness   Psalm 27:10   Psalm 25:16

                1 Samuel 12:22   Isaiah 41:10

                Romans 8:31–38   1 Peter 5:7

Depression	Psalm 34:17	Isaiah 40:31
	Isaiah 61:3	2 Corinthians 1:3–4
	Psalm 30:5	Luke 18:1
Anger	James 1:19–20	Romans 12:19
	Ephesians 4:26	Proverbs 25:21–22
	Proverbs 15:1	Ephesians 4:31–32
	Matthew 6:14	Matthew 5:22–24
	Psalm 37:8	Proverbs 14:16–17
	Proverbs 16:32	
Fear	2 Timothy 1:7	Psalm 23:4–5
	Psalm 91:10–11	John 14:27
	Proverbs 3:25–26	Psalm 31:24
	Isaiah 54:14	Psalm 27:1, 3
	Psalm 56:11	Romans 8:35–39
	John 4:18	
Courage	Psalm 27:14	Philippians 4:13
	Psalm 31:24	Isaiah 41:10
	Isaiah 43:2	Isaiah 40:31
Doubt about God	Mark 11:22–24	2 Peter 3:9
	Romans 4:20–21	Isaiah 59:1
	Luke 12:29–31	

Confidence	Philippians 4:13	Romans 8:37
	Hebrews 10:35–36	1 John 5:14–15
	Philippians 1:6	Proverbs 3:26
Desertion by loved ones	Deuteronomy 4:31	Isaiah 49:15–16
	Psalm 27:10	1 Samuel 12:22
	Matthew 28:20	1 Peter 5:7
	2 Corinthians 4:9	Deuteronomy 31:6
	Psalm 91:14–15	
The evil one	1 Peter 5:8-9	1 John 4:1-4
	James 4:7	Luke 10:17–19
	Hebrews 2:9, 14–15	Mark 16:17–18
	Ephesians 6:10–18	Matthew 12:28–29
	Colossians 2:10, 15	Proverbs 18:10
	Colossians 1:13	1 John 3:8
	Revelation 12:11	Romans 16:20
	2 Corinthians 10:3–5	1 John 2:13–14
Spiritual growth	2 Peter 3:18	Ephesians 3:14–19
	1 Peter 2:3–3	Colossians 3:16
	2 Peter 1:5–8	2 Corinthians 3:18
	2 Timothy 2:15	Psalm 92:12
	1 Timothy 4:15	Philippians 1:6, 9–12
	Hebrews 6:1	Ephesians 4:14–15
	Colossians 1:9–11	

Forgiveness	Jeremiah 33:8	1 John 1:9
	2 Corinthians 5:17	Hebrews 8:12
	Psalm 103:12	Mark 11:25
	Colossians 3:13	
Strength	Daniel 10:19	Isaiah 41:10
	Colossians 1:10–12	Philippians 4:13
	Isaiah 40:31	Ephesians 6:10
	Isaiah 40:29	
Controlling your tongue	Proverbs 18:21	Titus 3:9
	Ephesians 4:29, 31–32	Job 27:3–4
	Proverbs 24:28	1 Peter 2:23
	Luke 6:45	1 Peter 3:10
	Proverbs 13:3	

Prayer

St. Michael the Archangel,
defend us in battle.
Be our defense against the wickedness
and snares of the devil.
May God rebuke him, we humbly pray,
and do thou,
O Prince of the heavenly hosts,
by the power of God,
thrust into Hell Satan
and all the evil spirits
who prowl about the world
seeking the ruin of souls. Amen.

ABOUT THE AUTHOR

C rystalina Evert is the founder of Women Made New and co-founder of the Chastity Project. She is the best-selling author of *Pure Womanhood, How to Find Your Soulmate without Losing Your Soul,* and the curriculum *YOU: Life, Love, and the Theology of the Body.* Crystalina has spoken internationally to more than one million people about the virtue of chastity, healing, and God's plan for human sexuality and has made television appearances on MSNBC and the BBC. She has a weekly show on EWTN radio and has hosted several television series for teens and women on EWTN. She and her husband, Jason, have spoken at World Youth Day in Sydney, Madrid, and Poland and have been blessed with eight children.

ABOUT THE CONTRIBUTORS

Mother Angelica

Mother Mary Angelica of the Annunciation was born Rita Antoinette Rizzo on April 20, 1923, in Canton, Ohio. After a difficult childhood, a healing of her recurring stomach ailment led the young Rita on a process of discernment that ended in the Poor Clares of Perpetual Adoration in Cleveland.

Thirteen years later, in 1956, Sister Angelica promised the Lord as she awaited spinal surgery that, if He would permit her to walk again, she would build Him a monastery in the South. In Irondale, Alabama, Mother Angelica's vision took form. Her distinctive approach to teaching the Faith led to parish talks, then pamphlets and books, then radio and television opportunities.

By 1980 the Sisters had converted a garage at the monastery into a rudimentary television studio. EWTN was born. Mother Angelica has been a constant presence on television in the United States and around the world for more than forty years. Innumerable conversions to the Catholic Faith have been attributed to her unique gift for presenting the gospel: joyful but resolute, calming but bracing.

Mother Angelica spent the last years of her life cloistered in the second monastery she founded: Our Lady of the Angels in Hanceville, Alabama, where she and her Nuns dedicated themselves to prayer and adoration of Our Lord in the Most Blessed Sacrament.

Lisa Cotter

Lisa Cotter is a leading Catholic speaker and author known for her practical insights on relationships, femininity, and living life with excellence. She is the author of *Reveal the Gift: Living the Feminine Genius* and *Dating Detox: 40 Days of Perfecting Love in an Imperfect World*. She and her husband, Kevin, served FOCUS as a missionary family for more than ten years and are the cohosts of the popular *How-to Catholic* podcast. Lisa holds a degree in theology from Benedictine College and is finishing her master's degree in theology at Augustine Institute. She resides in Denver with her husband and their four children.

If you are interested in bringing Lisa to your next conference or retreat, you can visit her website, madetomagnify.com, or find her on Instagram, @lisaanncotter.

Cameron Fradd

Cameron Fradd is the founder of *Among the Lilies*, a podcast for woman "who are tired of pretending and ready to be real!" She speaks weekly to a growing community of women about being authentic and real. She speaks passionately about "the feminine genius" and believes that all women are beautiful and are wonderfully made. Cameron has an unshakable faith in our Lord and a deep desire to share her heart with others, especially women. Through her podcast, social media, and her speaking engagements, she is passionate about helping women discover their identity as beloved daughters of God. She spends most of her time raising and homeschooling her four beautiful, energetic children in Ohio, where she lives with her husband, Matt Fradd, with whom she coauthored the book *Restored: True Stories of Love and Lust After Porn*. With a smile always on her face and praise on her lips, Cameron presses onward one day at a time, uttering the words of her patron saint, Joan of Arc: "It was for this that I was born!" Learn more at https://www.cameronfradd.com/.

Catherine Hadro

Catherine Hadro is the founding host of *EWTN Pro-Life Weekly*, a global television show dedicated to the pro-life cause from a Catholic perspective. She now serves the Network as an EWTN news contributor and is a national Catholic speaker and writer. Throughout her career as a broadcast professional, Hadro has regularly interviewed top politicians, Church leaders, and cultural figures. Her reporting has caught the attention of outlets including *Vanity Fair* and *New York Magazine*. Her writings have appeared in the *National Catholic Register*, the *Washington Examiner*, and *RealClearReligion*, among other outlets. Catherine is a board member of the Obria Group. She is a graduate of Florida State University and resides in Virginia with her husband. You can find Catherine at CatherineHadro.com.

Sr. Bethany Madonna, SV

Sr. Bethany Madonna, SV, was raised in Melbourne, Florida. While attending the University of Central Florida, she had a profound encounter with the Lord, and this drew her heart toward the vulnerable unborn and their mothers. After her graduation in 2006, she worked for the Respect Life Office of the Diocese of Orlando before joining the Sisters of Life in 2007. Sr. Bethany made her final vows in 2015 and serves as the local superior and mission coordinator in Phoenix, where the Sisters accompany vulnerable pregnant women and also have a ministry of presence and evangelization on Arizona State University's Tempe campus. She is passionate about sharing the message of life and love.

About the ministry of the Sisters of Life
The Sisters of Life are a Catholic religious community of women founded in 1991 by John Cardinal O'Connor. Consecrated completely to Jesus, the Lord of Life, they commit themselves to the protection of human life and to the promotion of new life in Christ, acknowledging the sacredness of every person and sharing the good news of God's abundant mercy. In this way, they seek to help reveal to individuals their own innate goodness, the particular love God has for them, and the call to a life of abundant truth, joy, and hope. The Sisters are immersed in Eucharistic prayer within a vibrant community life, and their missions include caring for vulnerable pregnant women and their unborn children; inviting those wounded by abortion into the healing mercy of Jesus; fostering a culture of life through evangelization; retreat works; spiritual accompaniment of college students; and upholding the beauty of marriage and family life. Learn more at https://sistersoflife.org/.

Leila Miller

Leila Miller is a revert to Catholicism who has taught and written extensively on the Catholic Faith for the past twenty-five years. She has a passion for teaching the truths of our Faith in clarity and simplicity, and in recent years, she has focused on examining and exposing the devastating effects of divorce on children and on abandoned spouses. Because most Catholics are against divorce *in theory* but not *in practice*, the damage of divorce is rarely discussed and almost always discounted. Through her work, Leila gives the victims of divorce a voice they have been denied, while reintroducing poorly catechized Catholics to the teachings of Christ and His Church on the foundational topics of marriage and divorce.

Leila's books include *Primal Loss: The Now-Adult Children of Divorce Speak*; *Made This Way: How to Prepare Kids to Face Today's Tough Moral Issues* (co-written by Trent Horn of Catholic Answers); *Raising Chaste Catholic Men*; and *Impossible Marriages Redeemed: They Didn't End the Story in the Middle*. Leila's first blog, the popular *Little Catholic Bubble*, ran for eight years, and her current blog, as well as resources for marriage support, can be found at LeilaMiller.net. Leila and her husband, Dean, have eight children, ages thirty to twelve, and many grandchildren. They live in Phoenix, Arizona.

Joy Pinto

Joy Pinto is the executive director of Her Choice Birmingham Women's Center. She and her husband, Jim, have been married for forty-four years and have four children and seventeen grandchildren. Joy cohosts *At Home with Jim and Joy*, a weekly show on EWTN dealing with life, marriage, and family. Since 2009, Joy has been the director of a pregnancy help clinic in downtown Birmingham, encouraging women facing unplanned pregnancies to choose life and supporting them in that decision. Learn more at https://herchoicebirmingham.org/.

Dr. Kymberly Scipione

Dr. Kymberly Scipione is a mother of five and has been married to her husband, John, since 1998. They live in Aurora, Colorado. Kymberly completed two doctoral degrees and three master's degrees while being married and raising a family. She is a counselor and therapist trained in highly effective models of healing, and her private practice primarily focuses on women and trauma. She holds licenses in Colorado, Wyoming, and California. Learn more at https://www.drscipione.com/.

Sarah Swafford

Sarah Swafford is the founder of Emotional Virtue Ministries. She speaks internationally on a variety of topics, including faith, relationships, and interior confidence. Engaging audiences of all ages, Sarah shares her message at school assemblies, retreats, rallies, parishes, and conferences around the world, including FOCUS and Steubenville conferences in the United States and in Canada. She is the author of *Emotional Virtue: A Guide to Drama-Free Relationships* and is cohost of EWTN's *At the Heart of Relationships*. Sarah is a contributor to *Chosen* as well as *What We Believe: The Beauty of the Catholic Faith*, both published by Ascension Press. She resides in Atchison, Kansas, with her wonderful husband, Dr. Andrew Swafford, and their children: Thomas, Fulton, Cate, Kolbe, and John Paul. You can find more information about Sarah and Emotional Virtue Ministries at www.theswaffords.com.

Teresa Tomeo

Teresa Tomeo is an author, syndicated Catholic talk-show host, and motivational speaker with more than thirty years of experience in TV, radio, and newspapers; for twenty of those years, she was a secular reporter and anchor in the Detroit market. In the year 2000, Teresa left the secular media to start her own speaking and communications company, Teresa Tomeo Communications, LLC. Her weekday morning radio program, *Catholic Connection*, is coproduced by Ave Maria Radio in Ann Arbor, Michigan, and the EWTN Global Catholic Radio Network. It is heard on more than five hundred Catholic radio stations worldwide and on Sirius Satellite Network. Teresa appears frequently on the EWTN Global Catholic Television Network and cohosts the EWTN television series *The Catholic View for Women*. She is also a correspondent for *EWTN News In Depth*. As a deacon's wife, Teresa writes a column for Our Sunday Visitor's *The Deacon* magazine. In 2019, she opened her own Italy travel consultation company, T's Italy (TravelItalyExpert.com). Teresa has written more than ten books and is an international speaker, addressing media awareness and activism as well as sharing about her reversion to the Catholic Church. She resides in Southeast Michigan with her husband, Deacon Dominick Pastore. They travel the world giving marriage and diaconate couples' retreats.

Johnnette B. Williams

Johnnette B. Williams is the founder and president of Living His Life Abundantly® and Women of Grace®, a Catholic apostolate to women, whose mission is to transform the world, one woman at a time, through a program of spiritual formation. She is host of the international EWTN weekday television and syndicated radio programs *Women of Grace* and *Women of Grace Live*. A sought-after speaker, Johnnette presents on a variety of topics in various settings and geographic locations. She is also founder and president of the Benedicta Institute for Women®, whose mission is to identify, educate, develop, and train Catholic women to be active leaders and mentors in accord with their state in life. A mother and grandmother, Johnnette was married for thirty-three years until the death of her first husband. She married Jack Williams, general manager of EWTN Radio, in 2018. She is the author of several books and has developed study programs for women and teenage girls. For more information on her writings as well as the outreaches of Women of Grace®, visit www.womenofgrace.com.

Fr. Joseph Mary Wolfe, MFVA

Fr. Joseph Mary Wolfe is the chaplain of the Eternal Word Television Network, where he initially came to work in 1985 as an engineer. Two years later, he became one of the founding members of the men's community that Mother Angelica founded in 1987: the Franciscan Missionaries of the Eternal Word. The motto of his religious community is: *The lost I will seek out, the strayed I will bring back.* The friars do this by utilizing modern means of communication to reach millions of souls throughout the world.

Fr. Joseph was ordained to the priesthood in 1993 and often celebrates the daily televised Mass. He has produced a number of series featured on EWTN, including *Faith in the Heartland*, on the faith of farmers in his home state of Iowa; *The Church Universal*, on lay movements in the Church; and series on Fatima, Lourdes, and the Holy Land as well as a number of the prayers and devotions that regularly air on EWTN.